MAKING STORIES

MAKING STORIES

LAW, LITERATURE, LIFE

JEROME BRUNER

FARRAR, STRAUS AND GIROUX / NEW YORK

Farrar, Straus and Giroux
19 Union Square West, New York 10003

Distributed in Canada by Douglas & McIntyre Ltd.
Printed in the United States of America
First edition, 2002

Library of Congress Cataloging-in-Publication Data
Bruner, Jerome S. (Jerome Seymour)
    Making stories : law, literature, life / Jerome Bruner.— 1st ed.
        p. cm.
    Includes bibliographical references and index.
    ISBN 0-374-20024-6 (alk. paper)
        1. Narration (Rhetoric)   2. Narration (Rhetoric)—Psychological
aspects.   3. Law and literature.   I. Title.

PN212 .B78 2002
808—dc21

                                                          2001040888

Designed by Jonathan D. Lippincott

www.fsgbooks.com

1 3 5 7 9 10 8 6 4 2

IN MEMORY OF ALBERT GUÉRARD,
FRIEND, SCHOLAR, GENTLE TEACHER

CONTENTS

PREFACE

This brief book was born at the ancient University of Bologna, where I was invited to give the first *Lezioni Italiane* of the new millennium. The *Lezioni Italiane* are not "Italian lessons" in the conventional sense, but lectures given by a foreign visitor on a topic of his or her choosing. I chose a topic I hoped would reflect the ideals of Bologna's great university.

Ever since its founding in the twelfth century, Bologna has been a lively center of interpretive ferment, forever concerned with what words might mean, what texts are intended to signify, and how inscribed laws are to be interpreted in practice. But an interpretive stance is rarely welcome among established powers whose authority takes the world-as-is for granted. Bologna has had a long history of troubles with authority. The opening skirmish dates from the twelfth century, when Bologna's so-called *glossitiri* challenged conventional readings of Roman law as laid down in the authoritative Justinian Code six centuries before. Not context-sensitive enough was the Bologna claim. A century later a young student, Dante Alighieri, was suspended for writing an irreverent spoof on the interpretation of sacred texts. And more than a few times in later centuries, the university ran afoul of the Vatican on doctrinal matters. Bolognese interpretive skepticism flourishes to this day, nourished in our times by Umberto Eco's fresh approach to the semiotics of literary texts.

I could not resist this long tradition. Issues of interpretation have always fascinated me, and once again they are at the center of concern in both law and literature. Indeed, with the rebirth of cultural psychology, they have now become pivotal to our understanding of how we bring order and meaning to our lives.

I am grateful to the University of Bologna and to the Sigma Tau Foundation for honoring me with their invitation. Professor Paolo Fabbri of the university was not only a gracious host but a skillful and provocative chairman at the *Lezioni* in the Palazzo Marescotti. He, along with Umberto Eco and Patrizia Violi, helped make Bologna feel like where we belonged.

I must also express my gratitude to the New York University School of Law. My colleagues there have patiently instructed me over the last decade in the ways of the law, and granted me a term's study leave to reflect on what I'd learned—which led to the writing of this book. My colleague Professor Anthony Amsterdam should be held at least *partly* responsible for some of the views I express in these pages, particularly about the uses of narrative in the law. He has been a good friend, a generous teacher, and an unrelenting critic.

I have dedicated this book to the memory of Albert Guérard, novelist, scholar, and lifelong friend and teacher. It was he who led me to understand that psychology and literature have common roots, however different the fruits they bear.

Finally, I delight in expressing my gratitude to my wife and collaborator, Professor Carol Fleisher Feldman, whose wise and learned counsel has been indispensable. Her logistic acumen and dedication give grace and pattern to our lives.

Jerome Bruner
New York
June 2001

MAKING STORIES

ONE

THE USES OF STORY

Do we need another book about narrative, about stories, what they are and how they are used? We listen to them endlessly, tell them as easily as we grasp them—true or false ones, real ones or make-believe, accusations and excuses, we take them all in stride. We are so adept at narrative that it seems almost as natural as language itself. We know how to tailor our stories quite effortlessly to further our own ends (beginning with those sly twists that shift the blame for the spilt milk to a younger sibling) and know when others are doing the same. Our lives with stories start early and go on ceaselessly: no wonder we know how to deal with them. Do we really need a *book* about anything as obvious as narrative?[1]

I think so, and for the very reason that the subject is almost deadeningly obvious. For our intuitions about how to make a story or how to get the point of one are so implicit, so inaccessible to us, that we stumble when we try to explain, to ourselves or to some dubious other, what makes something a story rather than, say, an argument or a recipe. And though we may be crafty in shaping our stories to our own purposes, we still falter when trying to explain why Iago's tales, for example, undermine Othello's faith in Desdemona. We are not very good at grasping how story explicitly "transfigures the commonplace."[2] This asymmetry between doing and understanding is reminiscent of young kids being skillful at divvying up marbles but having little inkling of the mathematics that guides them—or, perhaps, of ancient Egyptians who fashioned the pyramids before understanding the geometry needed to do so.

What we know intuitively about stories is enough to get us through the familiar routines, but it serves us much less well when we try to understand or explain what we are doing or try to get it under deliberate control. It is like our early and naive grasp of space and number, celebrated by Jean Piaget. To get beyond implicitness and intuition, we seem to need some sort of outside hoist, something to take us up a level. And that is what this book is intended to be— a hoist up.

Why haven't there been more such hoists before? Are the underlying principles of narrative difficult to capture and formulate? Perhaps. We have some reason for dodging the issue, choosing to live with our shadowy intuitions instead. We surely haven't been without geniuses on the subject, though we've been inclined to ignore them as either arcane or too subtle by twice—like Aristotle, whose *Poetics* is full of stunning insights even for the contemporary reader. Why hasn't his concept of peripeteia been as widely taught to schoolkids as the geometer's less magical notion of the hypotenuse of a right triangle? A peripeteia, a sudden reversal in circumstances, swiftly turns a routine sequence of events into a story: a seemingly true-blue-English Oxbridge physicist turns out to have been leaking atomic secrets to the Russians, or a presumably merciful God all of a sudden asks the faithful Abraham to sacrifice his son Isaac. But not every upset of expectancy qualifies as a peripeteia. Is Aristotle's dissection of what makes a peripeteia work any less useful than Pythagoras's specifying that a hypotenuse is a line intersecting two others that form a right angle between them, with the square of the first equal to the sum of the other two squared? Why do we fob Pythagoras off on eighth-graders but never breathe a word to them about Aristotle on narrative? (We shall come to the niceties of the peripeteia presently.)

There may be something more than the subtlety of narrative structure that keeps us from making the leap from intuition to explicit understanding, something more than that narrative is murky, hard to pin down. Is it that storytelling is somehow not innocent, surely not as innocent as geometry, that it even has a wicked or immoral penumbra? We sense, for example, that too good a story is somehow not to be trusted. It implies too much rhetoric, something fake. Stories, presumably in contrast to logic or science, seem too susceptible to ulteriority—to special pleading and particularly to malice.

Perhaps this suspicion is justified. Stories are surely not innocent: they always have a message, most often so well concealed that even the teller knows not what ax he may be grinding. For example, stories typically begin by taking for granted (and asking the hearer or reader to take for granted) the ordinariness or normality of a given state of things in the world—what *ought* to prevail when Red Riding Hood visits her grandmother, or what a black kid *ought* to expect on arriving at a school door in Little Rock, Arkansas, after *Brown* v. *Board of Education* struck down racial segregation. And then the peripeteia upsets the expected sequence—it's a wolf dressed in Grandma's clothes, or Governor Faubus's Arkansas militia is blocking your entrance—and the story is on its way, with the initial normative message lurking in the background. Perhaps folk wisdom recognizes that it is better to let that normative message stay implicit rather than risk open confrontation about it. Would the Church want readers of Genesis to rail at the initial void that preceded heaven and earth, protesting "Ex nihil nihilo"? Thus literary theorists are wont to say that fictional terms only mean something in, but do not denote, the actual world.[3] Only lawyers or psychoanalysts would ask who the Wizard of Oz really stood for! Yet a young classics don at Oxford once told me scoldingly that Sigmund Freud's familistic realism had destroyed *Oedipus Rex* as a dramatic narrative for his generation. And I couldn't help complain back that what Freud had done for *Oedipus Rex* might have been even worse for family life offstage!

In any case, whatever the source of our odd reticence, we rarely inquire as to the shape reality is given when we dress it up as story. Common sense stoutly holds that the story form is a transparent window on reality, not a cookie cutter imposing a shape on it. Never mind that we all know, for example, that the worlds of good stories are peopled with free-willed protagonists of idealized courage or terror or malevolence who have to cope with obstacles to their desires that are preternatural, even preternaturally ordinary. Never mind that we know, again implicitly, that the real world is not "really" like this, that there are narrative conventions governing storied worlds. For we also cling to narrative models of reality and use them to shape our everyday experiences. We say of people we know in real life that they are Micawbers or characters right out of a Thomas Wolfe novel.

I recall returning to New York from a visit in Europe a month or so after the outbreak of World War II on a ship that departed from Bordeaux with a miscellany of American expatriates. A press account, perhaps in *The New Yorker*'s Talk of the Town, announced that the SS *Shawnee*, my ship, had arrived in New York the previous Wednesday with passengers who were like the cast of *The Sun Also Rises*, a then still popular Hemingway novel about the expatriate smart set. Having lived out the ten-day passage amid the heartbroken people on the boat—families separating for safety, merchants leaving their businesses behind, refugees fleeing the Nazis—I couldn't help being bemused by the ever-ready impulse to see life as imitating art. And I, too, was using a narrative in conceiving that journey: the *Shawnee*'s voyage as yet another enactment of the biblical Book of Exodus!

We should not write off this power of story to shape everyday experience as simply another error in our human effort to make sense of the world, though cognitive scientists are sometimes wont to do this. Nor should we shunt it off to the philosopher in the armchair, concerned with the age-old dilemma as to whether and how epistemological processes lead to valid ontological outcomes (that is, with how mere experience gets you to true reality). In dealing with narrative reality, we like to invoke Gottlob Frege's classic distinction between "sense" and "reference," the former connotational, the latter denotational, and we like to say that literary fiction does not refer to anything in the world but only provides the sense of things. Yet it is the sense of things often derived from narrative that makes later real-life reference possible. Indeed, we refer to events and things and people by expressions that situate them not just in an indifferent world but in a narrative one: "heroes" to whom we give medals for "valor," "broken contracts" where one party has failed to show "good-faith effort," and the like. Heroes and broken contracts can be referred to only by virtue of their prior existence in a narrative world. Perhaps Frege meant to say (he is ambiguous on the matter) that sense is also a way to give experiential shape, even to find what is referred to—as Dickens's fictional Mr. Micawber leads us to see certain real-life people in a new and different way, perhaps even to look for Micawbers. But I am getting ahead of myself. All I want to say for the moment is that narrative, including fictional narrative, gives shape to things in the real world and often bestows on them a title to reality.

So automatic and swift is this process of constructing reality that we are often blind to it—and rediscover it with a shock of recognition or resist discovering it with a cry of "postmodern rubbish!" Narrative meanings impose themselves on the referents of presumably true stories—for example, in the law, with an offense like "attractive nuisance," a tort judged to be present when somebody is lured into danger by an irresistible temptation created by somebody else. And so, by a court's judgment, your unfenced swimming pool is transformed from a place of innocent family pleasure into an actionable public menace, and you are liable. Irresistible temptation? Well, we cannot define it precisely, but we can illustrate by a line of legal precedent that tells supposedly similar stories. Anthropologists, to take another example, are becoming aware of the real-life political consequences of their own style of telling stories about primitive people—how, for instance, their talk about cultural autonomy may have provided justification, however cynically, for South Africa's apartheid policy.[4]

Only when we suspect we have the wrong story do we begin asking how a narrative may structure (or distort) our view of how things really are. And eventually we ask how story, *eo ipso*, shapes our experience of the world. Psychoanalysis, for example, asks how a patient's way of telling about her life affects how she lives it—Oscar Wilde's life imitating art transferred to the analytic couch.[5]

But let us stay a while longer with narratives of the imagination and with the question of how fiction creates realities so compelling that they shape our experience not only of the worlds the fiction portrays but of the real world. Great fiction proceeds by making the familiar and the ordinary strange again—as the Russian formalists used to put it, by "alienating" the reader from the tyranny of the compellingly familiar. It offers alternative worlds that put the actual one in a new light. Literature's chief instrument in creating this magic is, of course, language: its tropes and devices that carry our meaning-making beyond banality into the realm of the possible. It explores human plights through the prism of imagination. At its best and most powerful, fiction, like the fateful apple in the Garden of Eden, is the end of innocence.

Plato knew this all too well when he banned the poets from his republic. Tyrants knew this truth without Plato's instruction, as have all revolutionaries, rebels, and reformers. *Uncle Tom's Cabin* played as great a part in precipitating the American Civil War as any debate in Congress. Indeed, debates about slavery were banned from the floor of Congress after one of them led to a caning, and this lent the power of rarity to Harriet Beecher Stowe's remarkable novel, setting the travails of slavery in a narrative of suffering responded to by human kindness. And a century later, as we shall see, the novelists, poets, and playwrights of the Harlem Renaissance set the stage for the antisegregation ruling of the U.S. Supreme Court in *Brown* v. *Board of Education* by humanizing the plight of African-Americans living with the mockery of Jim Crow's separate-but-equal doctrine.

That classics don who complained to me about Freud's domestication of the Oedipus legend had a point—in turning *Oedipus* into a lesson, Freud had sapped the play's power to create imaginary worlds beyond psychoanalysis. For dramas like *Oedipus Rex*, even though they have the power to end innocence, are not lessons but temptations to reconsider

the obvious. Great fiction is subversive in spirit, not peda-
gogical.

I I

There seem to be two motives for looking closely at what
narrative is and how it works. One is to control it or to sanitize its effects—as in law, where tradition forges procedures
for keeping the stories of plaintiffs and defendants within
recognized bounds, or where legal scholars explore the kinship among claims that constitute a putative line of precedent (as when they set the limits on stories about "attractive
nuisance"); or as in psychiatry, where patients must be
helped to tell the right kinds of stories in order to get well.
The other motive for studying narrative is to understand it
so as to cultivate its illusions of reality, to "subjunctivize"
the self-evident declaratives of everyday life.[6] Its practition-
ers are literary—critics in all their guises and also creators,
even the occasional Peter Brook.

Until recent times, relations between these two differently motivated types, anti-fabulists and fabulists, have been
remote, each regarding the other as somehow soiling. But
the two have grown closer. Now there is a new and re-
spectable genre of legal scholarship, "law and literature,"
devoted to their shared dilemmas, with the novelist-critic
Janet Malcolm writing searchingly about law stories and
law professors like James Boyd White producing searching
essays on the metaphoric role of Heracles' bow in the law.[7]
But though they have grown closer, their kinship is not like

that between, say, biology and medicine or physics and chemistry—pure and applied or abstract and concrete. Yet the fabulists and anti-fabulists have at least come to know they must borrow from each other—though it is still obscure what coin is involved in the transaction.

Some points are becoming clearer. Literary narrative, to achieve its effect, must have its roots in familiar territory, in the seemingly real. Its mission, after all, is to make the familiar strange again, to transmute the declarative into the subjunctive.[8] Where better to do it, for example, than in the stifling familiar reality of the family, as with Eugene O'Neill's *Long Day's Journey into Night*, which begins in banal family routines and ends by plumbing the darkness of domesticated madness and decay? Or where better than in a courtroom, with its stately and ordered mise-en-scène and established procedures for exploring our obsessional search for order and justice?

Legal stories used in courts—as opposed to literary representations of them—however constrained they may be by procedural rules, also need to evoke familiar, conventional realities, if only to highlight the offending deviations from them. So law stories, too, draw on established narrative tradition. As Robert Cover remarked in his classic 1983 article, "Nomos and Narrative":

No set of legal institutions or prescriptions exists apart from the narratives that locate it and give it meaning. For every constitution there is an epic, for each decalogue a scripture. Once understood in the context of the narratives that give it meaning, law becomes not merely a system of rules to be observed, but a world in which to live.[9]

With due respect to judge and jury and to the procedural constraints of the law itself, cases are decided not only on their legal merits but on the artfulness of an attorney's narrative. So if literary fiction treats the familiar with reverence in order to achieve verisimilitude, law stories need to honor the devices of great fiction if they are to get their full measure from judge and jury. A novelist friend of mine spent months in Naples, getting a feel for its sights and smells while preparing to write a novel set there. A litigating attorney might do well to steep herself in novels and plays about the matter at hand before devising a strategy for her case—but more of that later.

I I I

I want to turn now to what Anthony Amsterdam and I have called the dialectic of the established and the possible.[10] We already know that law stories achieve legitimacy by invoking the past, by appealing to precedent. Surely this is no happenstance: we treasure predictability, even if we protect ourselves from it by guiles against boredom. We also know that while fiction may begin on familiar ground, it aims to go beyond it into the realm of the possible, the might-be, could have been, perhaps will be. We are all too ready to suspend disbelief, to embrace the subjunctive.

The canonical and the possible are forever in dialectical

tension with each other. And this tension especially impels and afflicts the third member of this book's subtitle: *Life*. For tales from life—autobiography, self-referent narrative generally ("self-making")—have as their purpose to keep the two manageably together, past and possible, in an endless dialectic: "how my life has always been and should rightly remain" and "how things might have been or might still be."[11]

A self is probably the most impressive work of art we ever produce, surely the most intricate. For we create not just one self-making story but many of them, rather like T. S. Eliot's rhyme "We prepare a face to meet / The faces that we meet." The job is to get them all into one identity, and to get them lined up over time. If we are to bring it off, we surely cannot abide by the enjoinder "Let not you and I inquire / What has been our past desire." For it is not just who and what we are that we want to get straight but who and what we might have been, given the constraints that memory and culture impose on us, constraints of which we are often unaware. To reconcile the mixed comforts of the familiar with the temptations of the possible requires an elusive art, as subtle as Proust's *Remembrance of Things Past*.

I introduce these matters now only to highlight how unsettled and unsettling narratives from life are. Law looks to the past for its legitimacy, literary fiction to the possible, bound only by verisimilitude, but what shall we make of the endless forms of narrative through which we construct (and maintain) a self? We shall have a chapter in which to consider such issues later.

IV

What are some of the useful things we already know (if only intuitively) about narrative, its nature and uses? Let me try to sketch out a few of them. Doing so might help us locate the gaps.

For one thing, we know that narrative in all its forms is a dialectic between what was expected and what came to pass. For there to be a story, something unforeseen must happen. Story is enormously sensitive to whatever challenges our conception of the canonical. It is an instrument not so much for solving problems as for finding them. The plight depicted marks a story's type as much as the resolution. We more often tell stories to forewarn than to instruct. And because of this, stories are a culture's coin and currency. For culture is, figuratively, the maker and enforcer of what is expected, but it also, paradoxically, compiles, even slyly treasures, transgressions. Its myths and its folktales, its dramas and its pageants memorialize both its norms and notable violations of them. Eve tempts Adam to taste of the fruit of the off-limits Tree of Knowledge, and *la vraie condition humaine* begins with the Expulsion from the Garden. One of my earliest memories is of childhood attempts to get my father to tell the "real story" behind Dürer's painting of the Expulsion, a black-and-white print of which hung in his study—why those two frightened figures were fleeing in such disarray. But I could see even then that his efforts to explain (mostly about man's disobedience to God) faltered when he got to the part about God forbidding Adam and Eve a knowledge of good and evil. In medieval and Renaissance Italy, the Sunday jester (made famous in our time by performances of the gifted mime Dario Fo) promoted just such faltering when he asked parishioners departing church after a sermon on the Fall, "What's so wrong with knowing about good and evil?" Why did the authorities abide such subversion by a clever jester on the very piazza that the cathedral fronted? Culture is not simply about the canon but about the dialectic between its norms and what is humanly possible, and that is what narrative, too, is about.

Michael Tomasello argues persuasively that what originally differentiated the human species from other primates was our extended capacity to read each other's intentions and mental states—our capacity for intersubjectivity, or "mind reading." It is a precondition for our collective life in culture.[12] I doubt such collective life would be possible were it not for our human capacity to organize and communicate experience in a narrative form. For it is the conventionalization of narrative that converts individual experience into collective coin which can be circulated, as it were, on a base wider than a merely interpersonal one. Being able to read another's mind need depend no longer on sharing some narrow ecological or interpersonal niche but, rather, on a common fund of myth, folktale, "common sense." And given that folk narrative, like narrative generally, like culture itself, is organized around the dialectic of expectation-supporting norms and possibility-evoking transgressions, it is no surprise that story is the coin and currency of culture.

What, then, is a story? Everyone will agree that it requires a cast of characters who are free agents with minds of their own. Given a moment to think about it, they'll also agree that these characters have recognizable expectations about the ordinary state of the world, the story's world, though these expectations may be somewhat enigmatic. And again, with a moment's thought, everybody agrees that a story begins with some breach in the expected state of things—Aristotle's peripeteia. Something goes awry, otherwise there's nothing to tell about. The story concerns efforts to cope or come to terms with the breach and its consequences. And finally there is an outcome, some sort of resolution.

One further component is usually offered as an afterthought when people tell you about story: there needs to be a narrator, a teller, and there needs to be a listener or reader, a told. Pressed on what difference that makes, we typically respond that a story expresses the narrator's point of view or perspective or knowledge of the world or, indeed, truthfulness or objectivity or even integrity, which may be hard to determine. "But if you find a story in a bottle that's been washed up on the beach," a fourteen-year-old said to me, "then there's no narrator." And after a short pause, "Wait a minute, that's stupid. Then you've got to figure out who the narrator was, which is even harder."

But I fear we are becoming too detached, concentrating on the abstract definition of a story. Let's look at a real one, a fictional tale worth a careful visit. The young captain in Joseph Conrad's "The Secret Sharer," standing a night watch alone off the Cochin China shore, is suddenly faced with Leggatt, climbing up from the sea on the Jacob's ladder carelessly left hanging by the previous watch. Leggatt is the escaped mate of "the Liverpool ship *Sephora*," just arrived and anchored in the lagoon awaiting a turn of tide. The captain's ship is at anchor outside the lagoon, readying for departure home. Leggatt, it turns out, strangled a seaman who'd failed to set a foresail in a wild storm during Leggatt's watch. Leggatt set the sail himself and saved the ship, but for his crime he was imprisoned in the *Sephora*'s brig, from which he escaped only nine hours earlier. Since that time he has been swimming in the sea—until he finally takes hold of the Jacob's ladder on the young captain's ship. That's the start: the unexpected.

Touched by Leggatt's confession and by their shared youth and inexperience, the captain takes him below, concealing him in his own quarters. "And I told him about myself. I had been appointed to take charge while I least expected anything of the sort, not quite a fortnight ago. I didn't know either the ship or the people. Hadn't had the time in port to look about me or size anybody up. As to the crew, all they knew was that I was appointed to take the ship home. For the rest, I was almost as much of a stranger on board as himself, I said. And at the moment, I felt it most acutely. I felt that it would take very little to make me a suspect person in the eyes of the ship's company."

The captain's ship finally sets sail for home. It is a dark night, a still one with scarcely a breath of air. The captain risks a first tack to bring the ship close to the shore so that Leggatt, the "secret sharer," may slip overboard unobserved to swim for land; then he orders the ship to the other, seaward tack. But has the maneuver left the ship dead in the water, fated to drift ashore? A wide-brimmed hat floating motionless on the water lets the captain know that his ship has come about and is headed out to safety—the hat had been his gift to Leggatt before he slipped overboard, given to shield him from the tropical sun. The captain moves to the taffrail, whence he can see his "second self [who had] lowered himself into the water to take his punishment: a free man, a proud swimmer striking out for a new destiny."

"The Secret Sharer" lends itself to many readings, as does much of Conrad. But however one reads it, the bones of its narrative structure hold it firm—the seemingly familiar detail in the busy readying of a ship for the home journey, but under the command of a new, inexperienced captain, a stranger, a would-be suspect to the ship's company. Then the disrupting arrival of Leggatt, a fellow "suspect," as it were. And, finally, there is the desperate, ambiguous tack inshore to let Leggatt slip into the water for his escape. Why does the captain hide the escaped Leggatt on board as a secret sharer? And why risk his ship and career, tacking so close to shore in such light air, when he knows that Leggatt was able to swim for hours on end getting from the *Sephora* to his own ship?

The outcome of the tale is also fraught with dilemma. Why is the young captain saved by that broad-brimmed hat, his token of generosity to the secret other? Narrative outcomes vary, of course, from the banal to the sublime; they may be inner, like a cleared conscience, or outer, like a safe escape. A wholesome setting-right of what the peripeteia put asunder may be the stuff of true adventure and other old-fashioned stories, but with the growth of the novel— and it is scarcely two centuries old—outcomes have taken an increasingly inward turn, as has literature generally. Story action in novels leads not so much to restoration of the disrupted canonical state of things as to epistemic or moral insights into what is inherent in the quest for restoration. Perhaps this is fitting for our times, though it is scarcely new. If it can be said, for example, that Thomas Mann's "Death in Venice" or *The Magic Mountain* gains its power from an inward resolution of the peripeteia, the same can be said of Sophocles' *Oedipus at Colonus* two millennia before. There may be many fashions in literary narrative, but deep innovations are scarce.

I've left out a final feature of stories, the coda, a retrospective evaluation of what it all might mean, a feature that also returns the hearer or reader from the there and then of the narrative to the here and now of the telling. In conversations I've had about what makes a story, few people mention this, and not surprisingly: perhaps they figure it's what comes *after* the story. A coda may be as explicit as an Aesop moral—"a stitch in time saves nine"—but it may also be like those final words of the young captain on Leggatt's escape ashore: "[M]y secret sharer . . . a free man, a proud swimmer, striking out for a new destiny." I, for one, will never know why Conrad had those words cross the young captain's lips. But so it is with codas. We are beyond Aesop: great narrative is an invitation to problem finding, not a lesson in problem solving. It is deeply about plight, about the road rather than about the inn to which it leads.

V

I taught a law-school seminar for nearly a decade with my colleague Anthony Amsterdam, its topic, roughly, "legal and other forms of interpretation." Amsterdam suggested we get our students to act out short narratives, working together in threesomes. We would assign a text for them to turn into a three-character play. One text was Genesis 22, the chilling tale of Abraham called to Mount Moriah and commanded by God to kill his young son, Isaac, to which Abraham agrees. God, convinced of Abraham's faith and loyalty, orders Abraham to desist and declares that henceforth the children of Israel will be his chosen. Three characters only: Abraham, Isaac, God.

One group of students performed God as a narcissist, Abraham as a fawning sycophant, things staying on course until Isaac, a funky kid, mocks God as a bully who's perpetrated a "contract under duress" for which he ought to be ashamed of himself—"And with all your power?" Another threesome had Isaac turn on God and his father for not consulting his mother, Sarah. Had God himself not blessed her with Isaac's birth in the lateness of her years? And now this? What kind of patriarchal arrogance was this, with God's little loyalty games? On they went. There was even one on what happened when God, like a positivist Austinian sovereign, made up his own rules with nothing to counter him. The seminar members served as critics as well as performers—a no-man's-land where lawyers spend much of their lives. What astonishing reach, that short tale from Genesis.

Students told us on several occasions that the little dramas their threesomes came up with often surprised them. I suspect their trips into playwriting on a theme made them conscious of how much more they knew than they thought they knew—and by what odd routes one comes to find out—not so much about law as about the power of acted-out, performed narrative to express ideas concealed in the everyday conventions of thinking and telling about things. Narrative seemed to open possible worlds, even in the reading of legal stories.

This brings us back to the odd dilemma of what we think we know about narrative. We know in our bones that stories are *made*, not *found* in the world. But we can't resist doubting it. Does art copy life, life art, or is it a two-way street? Even with fiction we wonder what a story is based on, as if it could not really be just made up. In Michael Riffaterre's deft words: "Fiction emphasizes the fact of the fictionality of a story . . . ; verisimilitude itself, therefore, entails fictionality."[13] But one might also add that verisimilitude in a made-up story is intensified by adhering (often slyly) to the rules of genre, and this suggests that our notions of reality are quite conventionalized. The hero-protagonist in a tragedy, for example, must suffer his downfall via the very virtues that make him a hero to start with, as Aristotle taught us long ago. So ingrained are such genre rules that fictional stories are made more lifelike simply by adhering to them.

Narrative, then, presents an ontological dilemma. Are stories real or imagined? How far have they leaped beyond our perception and memory of things in this world? And, indeed, are perception and memory yardsticks of the real, or are they artificers in the employ of convention? These questions will concern us more fully in Chapter 3, but the simple answer is that eyewitness and even vivid flashbulb memories serve many masters aside from Truth.

We try to take the sting out of this dilemma by gracefully admitting that, indeed, stories are always told from a particular perspective. The victor's tale of triumph is the loser's tale of defeat, though both were in the same battle. History, too, as historians have been insisting for generations, cannot escape the perspective that dominates its narrative telling.[14] Unmasking one perspective only reveals another. And however salutary this act may be as a critical exercise, it does not necessarily yield a supra-perspectival version of reality—if such a thing were ever possible. We comfort ourselves with the conclusion that it is the awareness of alternative perspectives, not the view from Olympus, that sets us free to create a properly pragmatic view of the Real.

The history of epidemics provides a gruesome example of the dilemma. Some eighty thousand more people die annually in the poorer than in the richer half of Britain's districts—far more than the total number who have died of AIDS since that disease first appeared there more than a decade ago. This massive death toll is not an epidemic, for poverty is not a component of the conventional story of epidemics—it is not "germy" enough to be included.[15] Then why don't we rewrite the history of epidemics to include the killer effect of poverty? The simple answer is that epidemic stories are told by medical epidemiologists, not by economists or reformers.

But while interpreting or altering the perspective of a story may afford temporary relief from the ontological dilemma, it creates one of its own. Whose perspective is the new one, and to what ontological or political end is its story mortgaged? Priests instructed the faithful of the medieval world in how Bible stories were to be taken, whether as *litteralis*, *metaphora*, *analogia*, or *anagogia*, whether literally, metaphorically, as an analogue, or in some mystical sense. Which was the real story remained moot, though medieval theologians had their insider quarrels on the matter. In our scientistic era, we would probably give the nod to *litteralis*: biblical archaeologists' finding the stones and bones of the battle of Jericho would make it "real."

A specialized form of the perspectival dilemma grows from the seemingly innocent fact—again one of those obvious, intuitive things we all know about narrative—that stories are communicated from person to person, their slant and believability depending on the circumstances of their telling. Like all speech acts, a story is a locution, but it also has a specific purpose: what a speaker intended by telling it to this listener in this setting. Philosophers refer to this intended objective of an utterance as its "illocutionary force."[16] Is the teller trying to reassure the hearer, defraud her, sell her a political bill of goods (as with those guilt-stricken anthropologists worrying about overselling the so-called simplicities of the primitive tribes in their field reports), or what? Even Scheherazade had an ulterior, "illocutionary" motive in telling her thousand and one tales to her new husband, the Sultan. He had routinely ordered his previous wives killed after the nuptial night. The newly wed Scheherazade knew a thing or two about how to keep story suspense unresolved!

Narrative intent is a particularly critical issue in the law, of course, since on its determination rest many legal decisions, like the determination of fraudulent intent. The New Critics ruled it out as irrelevant in literature: it mattered not *why* Herman Melville wrote *Moby-Dick* or Joseph Conrad "The Secret Sharer." Yet while I agree with their injunction, I want nonetheless to keep the issue of intent alive even in literature, for reasons I hope will become clear.

Stories, finally, provide models of the world—another of those intuitive matters we all know in our bones. Legal cases of the past are intended as precedents on which to model points of law in the present. Mythical stories in the ancient world, so celebrated in the scholarly work of Werner Jaeger and Jean-Pierre Vernant, were intended as models for virtues and vices.[17] To tell a story was to issue an invitation not to be as the story is but to see the world as embodied in the story. In time, the sharing of common stories creates an interpretive community, a matter of great moment not only for promoting cultural cohesion but for developing a body of law, the *corpus juris*.

What kinds of models are stories? How do they stand for the world beyond the particulars to which they directly refer? How does Conrad's sea-bound tale "The Secret Sharer" stand for events in the land-bound worlds of its readers? Surely, it does so principally as metaphor. And the haunting power of metaphor gives story its loft beyond the particular, its metaphoric loft.

But *what* do stories model metaphorically? Not the human act alone—Heracles cleaning the Augean stables or Prometheus bound to a rock. Stories are like doppelgängers, operating in two realms, one a landscape of action in the world, the other a landscape of consciousness where the protagonists' thoughts and feelings and secrets play themselves out. There on the landscape of action is a great fleet, prepared to sail on its punitive expedition to avenge Menelaus against Troy—windless. Agamemnon, its commander, is bade to sacrifice his daughter Iphigenia in return for fair winds. But now the landscape of consciousness: Agamemnon resolves his dilemma by convincing himself that his Iphigenia is proud to be sacrificed for such a high cause, while Clytemnestra, his wife, is convinced that Agamemnon is in the grip of self-aggrandizing self-deception. The fleet takes off, Troy is humiliated and sacked, and the world goes on. But Clytemnestra remains unforgiving, and the deadly clash at the level of consciousness gives the actions their dramatic impact—starting, perhaps, with Agamemnon's malice in carrying his Trojan prize, Cassandra, behind him in his chariot to his reunion with Clytemnestra; his vengeful murder at the hands of Clytemnestra, aided by her lover, Aegisthus; Clytemnestra murdered in turn by her son, Orestes; his sister Electra left finally to anguish. Even Aeschylus, chronicling the never-ending, self-renewing despairs of this doomed house of Atreus in his *Oresteia* trilogy, is left desperate. The best he can do, and that well into the third play, *The Eumenides*, is to have Athena herself intervene, proposing the creation of an Athens where juries (on the landscape of action) will keep vengeance (on the landscape of consciousness) from cycling out of hand yet again (on the landscape of action). "Phony," one of my students said. "What's she going to do with those Furies, get them to behave all of a sudden like Wellesley matrons at tea?"

It is part of the magic of well-wrought stories that they keep these two landscapes intertwined, making the knower and the known inseparable. In Aeschylus's drama, there is no objective stand-alone Iphigenia, however real-world her acts and their consequences may be and however terminal her sacrificial death. She does not quite fully exist outside the impassioned minds of Agamemnon and Clytemnestra, her parents, and when each of them is killed out of vengeance, she continues in the troubled mind of her sister, Electra. A narrative models not only a world but the minds seeking to give it its meanings. And this restless dualism is not confined to drama and fiction: it also plagues the lawyer telling his law stories and the autobiographer trying to construct a self.[18] But now we *are* getting too far ahead of the story!

V I

One last question. Why do we use story as the form for telling about what happens in life and in our own lives? Why not images, or lists of dates and places and the names and qualities of our friends and enemies? Why this seemingly innate addiction to story? Beware an easy answer! Even etymology warns that "to narrate" derives from both "telling" (*narrare*) and "knowing in some particular way" (*gnarus*)—the two tangled beyond sorting.[19]

For one thing, narrative gives us a ready and supple means for dealing with the uncertain outcomes of our plans and anticipations. As everyone from Aristotle to Kenneth Burke has noted, the impetus to narrative is expectation gone awry—peripeteia as the former called it, Trouble with a capital *T* as the latter did. Expectation is a characteristic of living beings, though it varies in sophistication and in the reach of time it encompasses. Its uniquely human expression is planning—devising appropriate, often contingent means for reaching the expected ends. A trio of distinguished scientists wrote a groundbreaking book in 1960, *Plans and the Structure of Behavior*, making a powerful case that the "plan" was *the* elementary neuro-psychic unit of human consciousness and action.[20]

Planning requires moderately well established expectations about how nature works and, even more important, how others will respond, for we rarely go it alone. Perhaps "the best laid plans . . . gang aft aglea," as Robert Burns's cautionary poem taught us in our school days, but the prosaic fact of the matter is that, thanks to the regularizing power of culture, our plans usually work out quite quietly and well. But it is our narrative gift that gives us the power to make sense of things when they don't.

We typically plan a quick trip to the grocer and succeed in getting what we set out to buy. *Ecco fatto*, as the Italians say: that's done. And we forget it. But I still remember an episode in Florence that formed the nucleus of what, by now, has grown into first-class kitsch historical narrative. My wife and I were on sabbatical there; she was preparing dinner. "Would you go down to Maurizio's and get us some of that nice chopped meat for an antipasto," she said. Off I went, down Via Masaccio to Maurizio's grocery. He was behind the counter, and I pointed to what I thought was our usual *salsa piccante* in the display case. "No, no, not that one. Signora la professoressa does not like that one," whereupon he dug into the refrigerator and produced my wife's favorite.

The historical narrative that sprouts from this little scene seems endless. It includes themes such as the centrality of the family in Italian culture and the dominance of the woman in family life; one can even trace the story back to Brunelleschi's extraordinarily elegant Ospedale degli Innocenti, the Foundling Hospital, built to protect mothers against the shame of illegitimate children. Transmuting Maurizio's countermanding act into an episode in Italian history, I can also include the then current battle of the beleaguered woman Minister of Health, trying to reform the high-handed mischief being done to health care by the big shots of the medical establishment—tellingly known as the barons, *i barone*. In any case, however lavishly I regularize that rather touching encounter over the *salsa* at Maurizio's, I am now prepared to be less surprised at whatever happens to me when shopping for groceries anywhere. Are stories part of our armamentarium for coping with surprise?

Obviously, our plans sometimes fail not just because we don't know enough but also because of the way we know things. And it is not just that we are "all too human" and shape our knowledge to conform to our wishes and fears. We are not good statistical machines, and are prone to inferential errors. These are fulsomely annotated in the literature on "human error tendencies"—errors in judging others, in making investment choices, in predicting outcomes generally. Stockbrokers have as many stories to "explain" why a stock they recommended didn't perform as they had about why it would when they first counseled you to buy it. One might even argue that the science of statistics was invented to save us from our predictive foibles. Even so, while no doubt we get carried away by our wishes and hopes, and no doubt our plans are badly pocked by the errors that both psychologists and economists celebrate, we learn to hedge and to play it safe. And our capacity for spinning possible stories guides us in doing so. For storytelling and story sharing make us deft in imagining what might happen if . . .

Let me add one interesting wrinkle. We humans are enormously specialized to adapt to the ordinary state of things around us—which psychologists have long called our "adaptation level," when we stop attending and go on automatic pilot. We go flat in response to monotony. But a century of brilliant neurophysiology has made it plain that human attention is also specialized to keep us vigilant about departures from the routine. An unexpected signal alerts us as nothing else does. A generation ago, indeed, neurophysiologists carried off Nobel Prizes for having established that sensory messages to the cerebral cortex from the outside world not only were transmitted by the usual sensory pathways, well known for a century, but were carried to the brain by an additional tract, the ascending reticular system, whose main function was to wake up the cortex, to clear it of the humdrum wave pattern into which it falls when the brain is comfortably bored.

What has all this to do with our addiction to narrative?

Narrative is a recounting of human plans gone off the track, expectations gone awry. It is a way to domesticate human error and surprise. It conventionalizes the common forms of human mishap into genres—comedy, tragedy, romance, irony, or whatever format may lessen the sting of our fortuity. Stories reassert a kind of conventional wisdom about what can be expected, even (or especially) what can be expected to go wrong and what might be done to restore or cope with the situation.

Narrative achieves these prodigies not only because of its structure per se but because of its flexibility or malleability. Not only are stories products of language, so remarkable for its sheer generativeness, permitting so many different versions to be told, but telling stories soon becomes crucial to our social interactions. How early the young child learns just the right tale for the occasion! Storytelling becomes entwined with, even at times constitutive of, cultural life.

V I I

Children enter the world of narrative early. They develop expectations about how the world should be, and their expectations show odd biases, as adults' do. And like adults, they are highly attuned to the unexpected, even attracted to the odd. Fascination with unexpectedness pervades their early play. For example, children easily grasp and delight in wordless dramas of the unexpected performed for them by adults, like peekaboo, and they do so before they have words enough to tell or understand stories. They delight in having these dramas repeated and, as in peekaboo, cherish the feigned surprise of their adult play partner.[21] But though ritual surprises delight them, the real thing may produce tears, which suggests a kind of narrative or theatrical precocity present almost from the start.

Let me illustrate how this narrative precocity expresses itself. Several years ago, I joined a few colleagues in studying the bedtime soliloquies of an irrepressible American child, Emmy, recorded by her parents on a hidden-under-the-bed tape recorder in the years before Emmy reached the age of three: tapes of Emmy musing to herself after she was alone in bed and before she fell asleep.[22] The soliloquies were not just about the routines of the day; she seemed drawn to the unexpected, to things that had surprised her or caught her unprepared. These little surprises would start her off on comments about how she had coped with their likes in the past or would cope with them tomorrow. So intent was she on getting her stories right that we came to believe her progress in acquiring language was driven by some sort of narrative energy. In some way Emmy seemed to know what a story required for its telling even before she had the grammar needed to tell it right. It was as if a narrative sensibility were guiding her search for the right syntactic forms.

Is this sensibility rooted in some uniquely human interest in the undoing of established expectancies by unexpected circumstances? Nothing quite like it is found in other higher primates, except perhaps in animals who have been domesticated and live with humans, as with the remarkable chimpanzee Kanzi studied so meticulously (and so hu-

manly!) by Sue Savage-Rumbaugh and her group in At-
lanta.[23] Not that the offbeat doesn't goad curiosity in lower
primates, only that they have limited interest in repeating
or ritualizing it, as we and our children do.

We seem, then, to have some predisposition, some core
knowledge about narrative from the start.

VIII

Let us return to what I referred to earlier as the "metaphoric loft" of stories. Little question that natural languages
are splendid instruments for representing and expressing
things in story form. Their commonsense grammar (what
linguists usually call "case grammar") easily takes note of
such narrative distinctions as the usual who did what to
whom, with what intent, with what result, in what setting,
along what time course, and by what means. There is no
known language without some case marking for such narrative essentials as agent, action, object, direction, aspect, and
the rest, codified in some version of what, as schoolkids, we
referred to as parts of speech. Case grammar makes narration easy in the same way that a shovel and spade make dig-
ging easy.

But you can't tell stories just by knowing case grammar!
They need something else, something that captures human
happenings over time. Some clever people have proposed
that there is a narrative grammar that captures the essential
nature of stories, and we'll visit them later. But the categories of such narrative grammars are not like the orderly

categories we use when we think of classes of abstract things such as prime numbers or powers of ten. Nor are they like the categories of actual objects such as "cats" and "dogs" that we can specify without regard to whatever a particular cat or dog is doing, whether meowing or barking. Narrative grammars, rather, are defined with reference to what's going on in the world of the story.

Kenneth Burke proposed more than a half century ago that, at a minimum, a story (fictional or actual) requires an Agent who performs an Action to achieve a Goal in a recognizable Setting by the use of certain Means—his dramatistic Pentad, as he called his grammar.[24] What drives a story is a misfit between the elements of the Pentad: Trouble. It can be a misfit between Agent and Action, Goal and Setting, any of the five elements of the Pentad. How could Agamemnon and Clytemnestra share a bed after he had sacrificed their daughter Iphigenia, the beloved fruit of her womb?

These imbalances are human plights, of course—or, in any case, we render them that way once we start communicating with each other about them. We generalize them, stylize them, make them congruent with what we know about the world. The Book of Exodus shaped my way of telling myself the story of those fleeing souls on the *Shawnee*, and telling myself that story shaped my very experience of that transatlantic crossing. And so it is with classic narrative plights. They become templates for experience: the mismating of awareness in marriage in Ibsen's *A Doll's House*, the awakening of a sense of injustice in Harper Lee's *To Kill a Mockingbird*, the pains and puzzles of growing up in whichever bildungsroman made a difference in our adolescent lives. What is astonishing about these narrative templates is that they are so particular, so local, so unique—yet have such reach. They are metaphors writ large: their loft is like the loft of myth.

It is the conversion of private Trouble (in Burke's sense) into public plight that makes well-wrought narrative so powerful, so comforting, so dangerous, so culturally essential. When Oliver Sacks takes us inside the mind of Temple Grandin, an intelligent autistic veterinarian, in his vivid "An Anthropologist on Mars," it is not just that he is bringing her to life. Metaphorically, he is bringing *us* to life by allowing us to see ourselves in her, to sense that her troubles with autism have the same shape as our own troubles in trying to figure out what others have on their minds. It is not so different from Harriet Beecher Stowe helping her contemporaries sense their own helpless plights in the struggles of the slave girl Liza in *Uncle Tom's Cabin*.

Now to narrative in law, literature, and life.

TWO

THE LEGAL
AND THE LITERARY

A legal story is a story told before a court of law. It tells about some act that is alleged by one party to have been committed by the other, an act that did damage to the accuser and that was in violation of a statute prohibiting such acts. The other party's story seeks to rebut the accusation by presenting another version of what happened or by claiming that the act in question neither harmed the accuser nor violated a statute.[1] Such opposing stories are at the heart of what we loosely refer to as "having your day in court."

The law has evolved over the centuries not only to render just and legitimate verdicts between two opposing narratives but to do so in a way that removes the risk of precipitating a cycle of revenge after the verdict has been pronounced. To achieve this dual objective, the courts must be accepted as authoritative and legitimate, and they must also be seen as fair and disinterested, capable of rising above the self-serving and adversarial narratives by which cases are presented.

A reputation for fairness obviously rests on a past record of fair verdicts. But it also depends on having litigation procedures that are commonly recognized as ensuring that standards of justice are being met. These procedures deal with, among other things, the kinds of legal stories permissible in court, their modes of telling, and how they shall be taken. Since they plainly cannot be taken for granted, how should they be taken, how constrained, limited, and evaluated? The answers to such questions will help to explain how ordinary stories get transformed into law stories.

We must look at the procedures by which law stories are analyzed legally and eventually judged from the bench or the jury box. First comes the crucial issue of "matters of fact" and "points of law." The law says that who did what to whom and with what intent are matters of fact to be established in accord with given rules of evidence. But whether or not an alleged act violates a particular statute requires interpreting a so-called point of law. And determining whether the act in question actually harmed the accusing party lies somewhere between the two. Like stories generally, then, law stories involve a subtle comparison of what was expected and what actually happened. The discrepancy between the two is then judged by criteria derived from statute and precedent.[2]

Take an ordinary legal face-off. An accuser claims that the accused promised to fulfill a contract—say, to build a wall by a certain date—and failed to do so: facts are cited and legal principles invoked. The accused then gives evidence to show that a "good-faith effort" was made to meet the contract's terms, the burden of which may be that forces beyond his control prevented him from doing so. The facts about dates and weather and work conditions in both stories are usually straightforwardly evidentiary; "forces beyond one's control" somewhat less so; and "good-faith effort" even more up for grabs, since the notion rests on circumstances and precedents.

Establishing the facts of the case is a process closely regulated by procedural rules such as the federal Uniform Rules of Evidence, as well as by court-administered oaths to tell the truth, backed up by threat of a perjury suit if false testimony is given. There are no comparable procedural constraints for judging the rightness of legal interpretation—only tradition as embodied in precedent. In offering an interpretation, a legal storyteller appeals principally to the likeness between her interpretation of the relevant facts in the present case and interpretations of what she claims are similar cases in the past. Establishing such lines of precedent is akin to locating a story in a literary genre, and lawyers (like literary critics) often exercise learned ingenuity in choosing their precedents. But ingenuity is constrained, again, by the lines of precedent that have been chosen in the past for like cases. While such lines are hardly wide-open to the legal storyteller, neither are they tight shut: respect is paid to both learnedness and legal ingenuity, even when the latter may seem rascally.

Lawyers know that even matters of fact filtered through the fine mesh of the Uniform Rules of Evidence are often open to interpretation. Take the "good-faith effort" in our contract case. May an attorney offer the argument "My client has never in thirty years of contracting been accused of an irregularity"? The opposing attorney will almost surely object to this statement on grounds that it is irrelevant. But will the jury be swayed by it even if the judge sustains the objection and orders the comment struck from the record? Besides, the relevance of established facts varies with the category they are put in. A pat on the shoulder, however friendly, is not an innocent, freestanding action in the light of a sexual-harassment charge.

Once a case has been decided, the decision may of course be appealed to a higher court—which offers further opportunity for legal storytelling. An appellate judge may offer a subsequent story to justify his holding in a case, particularly if he is overruling the lower court's decision. But such appellate-judge stories are devoted exclusively to justifying a legal interpretation, since they presume that "the facts of the case" have been settled in the lower court. Yet often enough, new interpretations alter the significance of previously established facts. When the Supreme Court, for example, with Justice Antonin Scalia writing the majority opinion, dismissed an appeal by a natural father for the right to visit his daughter living with her mother—a married woman with whom he had had an affair and who was back with her husband—the very fact of fatherhood changed in the Court's interpretation. "[T]he law, like nature," Justice Scalia wrote, "recognizes only one father," and, accordingly, the Court refused to admit in evidence genetic tests establishing the kinship of natural father and daughter![3]

One final point: lawsuits may not be mischievous; they must be consequential to the parties involved. An accuser must demonstrate a legitimate standing in the matter at issue for her complaint to be heard by a court. For example, a California resident's suit against New Jersey highway patrolmen for their alleged practice of "racially profiling" highway arrests will not be heard unless the Californian suffered demonstrable harm. A citizen of New Jersey suing on like grounds might be heard, however, since she has standing in the eyes of the New Jersey law. A would-be litigant must have not only standing but grounds. You cannot get an injunction against the city of New York to prevent its planting banal species of trees. You need grounds to get this done, and these are established in statutes or writs setting forth what violates "state interest"—rather like a sum of actionable peripeteiae. All this—standing and grounds taken together—means that law stories are always, and are guaranteed to be, highly consequential to the parties engaged. They matter, and their believability matters. It is in no sense playful storytelling.

Another thing unique to law stories is the way in which they are told. Attorneys sum up the whole story in their closing arguments before the court, after having called witnesses of their own choosing to testify on behalf of their client's case. In some jurisdictions, the judge may also summon witnesses, "friends of the court," *amici curiae*. Witnesses are akin to actors in a staged drama, and adversary lawyers match their witnesses against each other. We can see why playwrights find the courtroom a congenial mise-en-scène or why lawyers ham it up when they can.

I I

Given all that's been said thus far, it's not surprising that law stories are distrusted—not only by the parties facing off but by those who must judge between them. And with good reason, for everyone knows that however principled they are in their quest for justice, lawyers tell stories committed to an adversarial rhetoric. And everyone knows too that, despite the procedural limits designed to contain their rhetoric, that rhetoric influences the final judgment. Such matters often become sticky and technical, as in lawsuits that arise over "tailoring," where one party claims that a witness gained an advantage by being called to testify late in a trial and was therefore able to hear testimony he might not otherwise have heard.[4] It is not enough that the Uniform Rules of Evidence ban hearsay and the testimony of spouses and affected family members and the like. Law stories simply are not, have never been, and probably will never be taken at face value. So there must be something profound about our confidence in how the legal *process* sanitizes them.

One element of that confidence is our faith that confrontation is a good way to get to the bottom of things. To honor that faith, standard legal procedures offer opportunities for adversary attorneys to cross-examine each other's witnesses, to challenge their stories, and to propose plausible alternatives. They also ensure that the confrontation will stay within courteous limits by restricting what witnesses may be asked and how they may be challenged. Opposing attorneys may object to certain questions or answers, but the judge has the last word—presumably in the higher interest.

And this interplay between self-interested partisanship at the bar and dispassionate proceduralism on the bench seems to be what nourishes our sense that the contending parties have had "their day in court." It also provides the drama in those courtroom scenes so dear to novelists and playwrights.

But while confrontation and cross-examination may be the most dramatic elements in reconciling people to the rhetorical rough-and-tumble of law stories, another matter that goes beyond these precautionary procedures may be equally important. It lies at the heart of common law, which will be our principal concern here. It is the concept of precedent: the idea that a judicial decision in the present case should be reached on the basis of decisions in like cases from the past, a doctrine referred to reverently as *stare decisis*. A law story prevails hardly by dint of its rhetoric but, rather, by establishing that there were precedents that match it.

To prevail, legal stories must be devised with a sharp eye to discerning which cases in the past were similar to the present one and judged in a manner favoring one's side. Appropriate precedents are templates, as it were, for guiding an attorney in organizing a story of the present case. He or she is well advised to root the case *sub judice* in a line of favorable precedent.

To sum up, law stories are narrative in structure, adversarial in spirit, inherently rhetorical in aim, and justifiably open to suspicion. They are modeled on past cases whose verdicts were favorable to them. And, finally, they are really consequential, since the parties involved must have standing and must be directly affected by the outcome. Narrative, adversarial, rhetorical, and suspicious! And while law stories are protected by procedures designed to overcome the blemishes, few believe that the protection is complete. So, we may properly ask, why do people have such confidence in the legal system as, plainly, most do?[5] What gives them confidence that the gold of truth and justice can be filtered from the rhetorical dross of law stories?

The answer is law's legitimacy. But legitimacy comes from more than sheer procedural acumen, or from the genius of a past-preserving *corpus juris*, or from the stability-seeking doctrine of *stare decisis*. Law's legitimacy in contemporary democracies rests on the established belief that you will have your day in court and be dealt with as others have been before you under comparable circumstances. And it is further ensured by ritualization, an endlessly fascinating phenomenon whose full explication would take us too far beyond our concerns here. But several points about ritual's judicial form are worth noting.

Legal proceedings are, for one, ritually solemn. Laughter is regarded as inappropriate unless it is intentionally initiated from the bench, which is rare. Respect for the presiding officer of the court is expressed in such ritual commands as "Order in the court!" when an inadvertent disturbance occurs and by the enforced rule that the audience rise when the judge enters or leaves the courtroom. The "Oyez" of the clerk in announcing the court to be in session adds to the ritual atmosphere, and the stilted language of legal doctrine adds still more. The law, critics like to point out, is strong on ritual self-congratulation about its "internal morality," as Lon Fuller has called law's procedural requirements: that a law should be accessible in advance of its application, that it should be patently free from arbitrariness, and on down Fuller's famous list of eight criteria of a legitimate law and its application.[6] Never mind that the history of appellate law speaks to their being frequently disregarded: the authority of a judge is not thereby affected. While a judge's verdict is subject to appeal, of course, he or she is not legally liable for errors of judgment: judges enjoy immunity from prosecution for their opinions, even when those opinions are reversed by a higher court, even when they can be shown to have caused demonstrable harm to a litigant. Perhaps such immunity is a necessary condition for any judicial system, but let it be noted that it is unique to the judicial system, with no legitimized parallel elsewhere in society. David Kertzer sums it up well: "Successful ritual . . . creates an emotional state that makes the message uncontestable because it is framed in such a way as to be seen as inherent in the way things are . . . beyond debate."[7]

The historical record of courts adds still more glamour to their ritual importance. Democratic legal systems are symbols of a successful struggle against tyranny and autocratic arbitrariness, after all. We legitimize their rituals in the light of that history, however dimly it may be known to the public. And rootedness in a tradition is surely a necessary if not a sufficient feature of acceptable social ritual.[8]

So ritually effective is the system of law that courts rarely need to invoke their police powers to enforce their decisions and decrees. The court system, to cite a commonplace, can afford to be the "weakest branch of government." Given the struggles against tyranny that brought most legal systems into being, they do well to use their police powers lightly! Their rituals serve them well.

The crucial, steadying role of ritual in resolving disputes is usually emphasized by pointing to its conspicuous importance in the "legal systems" of virtually all preliterate societies. A number of brilliant and detailed accounts have been written of how this is accomplished in different cultures, particularly how rituals of adjudication manage to stem cycles of revenge. One of the most gripping is by the renowned English anthropologist E. E. Evans-Pritchard in his classic study of the Azande in central Africa, and equally compelling studies have come from such other distinguished students of simpler cultures as Clifford Geertz (comparing Moroccan, Indonesian, and Indian cultures), Max Gluckman (observing Barotse adjudication in Africa), Sally Falk Moore (looking at property disputes among the Chagga on the slopes of Mount Kilimanjaro), and Donald Brenneis (trying to fathom dispute management among a transplanted Hindu Indian community in Fiji). What one learns from these studies, as Oscar Chase has remarked, is that the rituals used, however bizarre they may seem to the outsider, are deeply embedded in the culture's general practices and are typically made to seem congruent with local "common sense."

Our Western judges wear black priestly robes, signifying their metaphoric elevation beyond the contentiousness of everyday life. Among the Azande, judges use oracles: not conventional ones as we understand the term, but chickens fed a specified dose of specially prepared poison by an expert at this *benge* ritual, as it is called; if a chicken perishes, the accused is guilty as charged, and if it survives he is innocent (*he*, for women are not included in this trial process). Bizarre as this may seem, the Azande have astutely incorporated the *benge* oracle into their way of life. After all, good fortune and ill fortune can be traced to the world of spirits and witchcraft, as can the survival of a chicken submitted to a standard dose of poison. Besides, it takes *two* chickens dead to prove guilt, and one may appeal afterward to the chief's *benge* oracle if one is not satisfied with the outcome of the first trial-by-poison. And matters can be settled even before that appeal is granted, for Azande guilt does not imply an intent to do harm: the accused party may simply have been unwittingly possessed by evil spirits. Under the circumstances, retribution and vengeance take on a somewhat less embittered (or differently embittered) character. It is plain that the system works surprisingly well for the Azande: it achieves a commonsense justice, and, particularly, it manages to keep vengeance in hand. And they express satisfaction with it, even complaining that the British who came in during the nineteenth century did rather silly things in trying to alter it.[9]

III

I believe there is something more to the legitimation of legal storytelling than trust in judicial procedures, rules of evidence, and ritualization. I believe more and more that the use of recognizable, garden-variety narrative in legal pleading gives us assurance that the "law still belongs to the people," as it were, not just to hateful lawyers and stolid judges with their obscure talk. "Liars all," a cabdriver once said to me as he drove me to New York University Law School's Vanderbilt Hall after I had assured him that I was not a lawyer. And then, "I guess they're needed, if they'd only help the right people, only listen to them." Narrative pleading, I have increasingly come to believe, remains Everyman's portal into the arcane realm of law. It is the common sense of justice.

But attorneys and judges do not like being complimented as great storytellers. They work hard to make their law stories as unstorylike as possible, even *anti*-storylike: factual, logically self-evident, hostile to the fanciful, respectful to the ordinary, seemingly "untailored." Yet in pleading cases, they create drama, indeed, are sometimes carried away by it.

Law's literary cousins live a quite different life. As any writer or playwright will assure you, his task is to imagine, to explore possibility. But to do that, he must first establish a familiar "reality," given that his mission is to estrange it, to render it alien enough to make imagined deviations from it seem plausible. In Ibsen's *A Doll's House*, for example, Nora's dramatic revulsion becomes credible only against the deadening banality of her preternaturally ordinary husband. It is the playwright's genius to have captured both the tedium of her life and her rebellion against it. The challenge of literary narrative is to open possibilities without diminishing the seeming reality of the actual. The narratives play variations on the plights portrayed in conventional literary genres yet honor the reality of those plights. At their most venturesome, they even generate new genres to achieve their ends—as did Laurence Sterne or James Joyce, with his self-styled epiphanies of the ordinary.

Legal stories strive to make the world seem self-evident, a "continued story" that inherits a legitimated past, while literary fiction evokes familiar life with the aim of disturbing our expectations about it the better to arouse our sense of what might lie beyond it. Literature mimics accepted reality with its wiles for creating verisimilitude; law does it by citing the *corpus juris* and abiding by precedent. Can one mix the two? We are told that when in ancient times there were no plays by Aeschylus, Sophocles, or the other greats, Athenians often repaired to the law courts. What did they there?

Many centuries later, the emperor Justinian was bound and determined to gather records of legal opinions from every corner of Rome's vast empire. He wanted his commission of lawyers and professors to sort them into tidy legal categories, to establish a code of justice that was everywhere the same and everywhere free from local drama: a universal code, he felt, would serve justice better. Perhaps in that troubled sixth century, with Rome trying to come to terms with its new barbarian diversity, law risked becoming too erratic, too much like theater and tale-telling (at least in Justinian's eyes). He wanted Roman law to be as unsurprising, undramatic, unlocal as possible, and to let everyone know that they lived under the uniform and perduring shield of Rome, *status populusque romanum*. Besides, the police power of the Roman army was so thinly spread across a realm with a three-thousand-mile perimeter that Justinian could afford no local surprises! He wanted law courts, not military police. (Similarly, latter-day Hebrew law originated, according to Robert Cover, in the diaspora after the destruction of the Second Temple, when it became necessary to contain the unpredictability that inevitably followed the demise of compassionate propinquity once the Hebrews had been scattered.[10] Law, in the proper sense of a code, comes into being only through *jurisgenesis*, as Cover calls it, when diaspora destroys face-to-face intimacy in a community.)

Justinian's famous Code never quite worked as uniformly as intended. Perhaps uniform codes never do; perhaps *jurisgenesis* never fully assuages the human yearning for local and intimate drama. It is somehow not enough for law to be simply the will of the sovereign, unrelated to popular morality in the legal positivist's sense. There seems always to be some local, inner point of view that wants minding. Culture, as Clifford Geertz rightly puts it, is always local, always particular, however universal its aspirations.[11] And for all that we proceduralize and sanitize the law, it cannot be effective when it is seen as incongruous with the local culture. Indeed, as I shall relate presently, precisely for this reason common law has traditionally claimed its superiority: it looks for continuity in the particulars rather than for universality by deduction from abstract legal rules. Is this why law cannot do without narrative?

There seems to be a perpetual tension between the view of law as *non sub hominen sed sub legem et Dei* and the more humane doctrine that justice must be tempered with mercy (or, at the other extreme, hardened by righteous anger). Can

law, with its dependence on narrative, however constrained
by procedures, ever fully escape this tension?

IV

Let us consider literary narrative in this context, then, with
its intent to subvert familiar expectations while respecting,
even vivifying reality. At the outset, perhaps it should be
taken as a compliment to literature when folk wisdom pro-
claims the truth to be stranger than fiction. It suggests that
literary artifice is getting away with its "rhetoric of the
real." Literature achieves this success by artful tropes and
the magic of plotting, its devices for both depicting and
transforming reality believably. Good news when the storyteller's reality seems less strange than everyday life!

Literary narrative "subjunctivizes" reality, as I suggested
earlier, making room not only for what is but for what
might be or might have been. A subjunctivized world,
though it may not be comfortable, is provocative. It keeps
the familiar and the possible cheek by jowl. To read the
stories in Joyce's *Dubliners* is to be immersed in possible
worlds that are deeply familiar. So why do we want, seek,
even find renewal in these unhinging subjunctivized worlds
of fiction? Our brain has as many connections among its
neurons as there are stars in the Milky Way; it lives and
grows by being in dilemmas: we fall asleep when there is
not enough to keep those neurons at work, fail to develop
our powers.

It is difficult to resist the conclusion that our all-too-human preoccupation with the unexpected in the familiar reflects our evolution as a culture-dependent species. It suits us well (if sometimes uncomfortably) in our coping with the uneasy balance of custom and innovation that characterizes the symbolic world of culture. For while human culture generates the predictability of custom through its institutions (including its laws), it notoriously produces ambiguities and antinomies at a rate and in a manner found nowhere else in the animal kingdom. Indeed, one increasingly widespread view is that culture is as much a prod to the development of human cognition as human cognition is to the development of culture.

Yet narrative requires buffers that guard the hearer or reader against the terrors of unlimited possibility—buffers like Perseus's mirroring shield that keeps him from being turned to stone should he look at Medusa directly. He finally takes her measure in the mirror of his shield—and severs her head with a well-aimed thrust. Literature's tropes are Perseus's mirroring shield: they save us from the full terror of the possible. Each age invents its own shield of Perseus so that it may look on the possible without being turned to stone. Herman Melville confided to his friend Nathaniel Hawthorne that in *Moby-Dick* it was Christianity he had in mind as the white whale, harpooned finally by Queequeg, the most pagan of that all-pagan crew in the slender whaleboat that goes out from the solid *Pequod*, a ship from Puritan New Bedford. Captain Ahab's pagan crew, *in nomine diaboli*? Is the sea adventure of that astonishing book what keeps us from being turned to stone by Melville's anti-Christian message? Is it Emma Bovary's ordinariness that

saves us from the shock of Flaubert's tale of the possible im-
possibility of marriage?

V

In time, the altered narrative sensibility produced by literature comes to affect how lawyers tell their legal stories and
how judges put them into legal categories. Eventually well-
wrought literary narrative works its way, sedulously, into the
corpus juris of past legal decisions, its presence there provid-
ing further inducement to the lawyer to make his or her law
stories more like literature.

I want to offer an example of how literature finds its
way into the law's *corpus juris* and inscribes its possible
worlds on it. It is the well-known school-desegregation case
decided by the U.S. Supreme Court in 1954, *Brown* v. *Board
of Education.* The canonical expectation or norm at issue in
that case was the Constitution's guarantee of equal protection under the law for all citizens, regardless of their race,
color, or creed. The question before the Supreme Court was
whether the equal-protection guarantee was violated by the
practice of *de jure* racial segregation in local school districts,
even if such segregated schools could be shown to be equal
in terms of dollar outlay and other "objective" factors. The
matters of fact in the case had long since been settled: *de
jure* segregation admittedly existed, and the defendants offered material evidence that the segregated schools were
equal in facilities though separate in fact.

The real question before the Court was an interpretive

one based on narrative kinship. Should *de jure* segregation be interpreted as a violation of the equal-protection clause of the Fourteenth Amendment of the U.S. Constitution? The answer to that question depends on how one interprets equal protection. Specifically, do racially "separate but equal" schools for black and white children meet the canonical standard of equal protection for all?

Now turn to the precedents. The Supreme Court had decided in 1896 in *Plessy* v. *Ferguson* that the provision of "separate but equal" railroad cars for traveling blacks and whites met the standard required by the Fourteenth Amendment. If the railroad-car standard also held for schools, then there was no case. All that needed to be shown was that *de jure* segregated black schools were just as well supported materially as white ones.

But in the half century following *Plessy*, many things had changed in American narratives about race. There had been a world war against Hitler and Nazi racism. Segregation of any kind smacked of concentration camps and the Nuremberg decrees. Perhaps just as important, there had been an enormous literary change as well, an "inward turn" in narrative. Even for separate-but-equal Jim Crow railroad cars, the question had become a subjective one: How did it feel to be shunted into a separate railroad car or sent to the back of the bus? What did it do to one's self-respect and, critically, to one's will to learn and develop? The parallel question regarding schools became, What does segregation do to black children's view of themselves, their self-esteem, their readiness to learn? The landscape of consciousness had become part of the narrative of equal protection.

In the years after *Plessy*, subjective themes of this nature were at the center of powerful (and successful) poetry, plays, and stories written by widely read black authors like Langston Hughes and Richard Wright. Their voices became part of the American literary tradition of consciousness and protest. They had plenty to say about what it felt like to live Jim Crow.

Their voices can be heard in the background of the 1954 Supreme Court opinion that finally overruled the separate-but-equal standard of *Plessy*. The Harlem Renaissance had given equal protection its subjective story—if not in the *corpus juris*, then in the popular imagination. In the *Brown* opinion, that subjectivity is explicitly mentioned, but it had begun to make its presence felt in the appellate litigation that preceded the Supreme Court decision. I testified as an *amicus curiae* in the 1952 *Gebhart* v. *Belton* Delaware appeal that eventually led to *Brown*, and my testimony concerned the damage to self-respect that school segregation was known to produce in black children, equal funding notwithstanding. The law story I offered as a witness was as prototypically law story as it could be. I'd had witness coaching down to the last detail from the attorneys of the NAACP Legal Defense and Educational Fund who were masterminding the nationwide legal campaign against *de jure* school segregation.

Imagine my astonishment, then, when the attorney representing Delaware's segregated school system chose to forgo cross-examining me! "What was there for him to say that would be palatable," said Louis Redding, my lawyer-coach, when I expressed my surprise. The *corpus juris* hadn't yet changed. But three years later, the Supreme Court set forth its unanimous decision in *Brown* v. *Board of Education*, with its famous footnote citing the joint views of our committee of expert witnesses who had participated in the appeal cases that led up to *Brown*.

Should we conclude that the *Brown* decision finally caught up with American culture's changed narrative about racial discrimination? Well, that is not clear. The inward turn was not the only part of the story. The issue remained (and remains today) what constitutes the appropriate remedy for the damage done by racial segregation. And there is no settled narrative on that issue—neither popular, nor literary, nor legal. Since *Brown*, steady efforts have been made to give the segregation story a new reading, this time centering on remedy, or on "affirmative action" favoring those previously discriminated against. But the principal new story is about protecting *whites* against the desegregation remedies mandated by courts and legislatures, with individual whites depicted in the new narrative as the victims—a certain person named Bakke refused admission to medical school in California, or a particular Miss Hopwood entrance to a state university in Texas.

The courts, in duly responding to this newly minted story about protecting whites against desegregation measures, have made it part of the *corpus juris*. *Hopwood* v. *Texas* (Fifth Circuit, 1996) ruled, for example, that educational institutions are hereafter forbidden to use any information about race or color in admitting students— "color-blind" is the term. The controlling image is of Justice with her blindfold back on, presiding over a "level playing field" where blacks and whites are equal—and *Brown* is cited as having guaranteed that it was so! Never mind that everybody knows, whether from statistics or everyday observation, that the playing field is *not* level.

The narrative dialectic in progress is curious. The inward turn of literary narrative about race went a long way toward changing the legal interpretation of equal protection when it was given a subjective dimension in *Brown*, and that opinion was widely hailed as a great and humane step forward. But no culture is about just one story. A dialectically contrary one quickly arose: the story of the black being given "unfair advantages," a story with roots in the Reconstruction period after the abolition of slavery, when Northern commanders of occupation troops in the Southern states of the old Confederacy even appointed some black governors. This time, a revenant legend rather than a new literary movement provided a narrative for transforming the line of precedent into one that fit a new mood of economic insecurity in the white middle class. And there followed a series of cases, beginning in 1978 with the *University of California Board of Regents* v. *Bakke*, in which the courts first imposed a strict test-score admission criterion and then enunciated a "color-blind" criterion, as in *Hopwood* v. *Texas*.

How might the "story" of segregation and desegregation have been told in the light of what we've learned since? How might Thurgood Marshall have argued the case before the Supreme Court in *Brown* v. *Board of Education* so as to forestall the new narratives that marked subsequent cases and weakened *Brown*'s impact? Should he have given less emphasis to the "psychological story" of *de jure* segregation diminishing the self-regard of African-American children? In the story at the time, it certainly made sense as a narrative instrument against the *Plessy* doctrine of separate but equal. Yet in a recent book in which nine law professors have a go at rewriting *Brown*, none of them uses the psychological evidence contained in the opinion's famous Footnote 11, which set forth the conclusion about the devastating effects of segregation on schoolchildren. Perhaps, as one reviewer of the book has argued, the psychological evidence was irrelevant and ultimately the authority of *Brown* resides "in the recognition that the decision accords with our deepest constitutional values."[12] Indeed, narratives change to reflect the spirit of their times.

VI

The tension between what is possible and what is established is built into the texture of Anglo-Saxon common law, into the very system of writs that was its origin—a system compelling enough to have lasted from the twelfth into the nineteenth century. A common-law writ, to put it simply, is a plot summary of an actionable offense against what is customary and established. Before the system buckled under its own excessive particularity, there were some 357 of these writs. They mostly concerned offenses against property rights, inheritance customs, and rules of trespass, and they were not set forth in general terms or by definition but, rather, illustrated by cases on record.

At first, writs were issued by local courts when a party

complained that he had been harmed in some recognizable way by another's acts. They were even issued on a complaint that the accused had acted in a way that disturbed "the King's peace." The accused party was compelled to appear before the court to defend himself, and under the scrutiny of the court accuser and accused faced each other and told their stories, or their lawyers did if they could afford them. The officiating magistrate, with or without a jury, then rendered a verdict.

In time, writs became more uniform and standard, once Royal Chancery Courts became strong enough to impose their power. Eventually they became so conventionalized that they even bore titles, like novels. One from the eighth edition, published in 1755, of Anthony FitzHerbert's standard and indispensable compilation the *New Natura Brevium* bears the euphonious title *moderata misericordia*.[13] As with writs generally, it scrupulously avoids enunciating any general legal principles, though its obvious purpose was to protect people from penalties that were incommensurate with their wrongdoings—excessive fines, overpriced penalties for nonperformance of contracts, whatever. In lieu of principles, previously decided cases were cited. FitzHerbert's citation footnotes are copious, intended to instantiate *moderata misericordia* rather than to define or generalize it. And, of course, given this procedure, the writ was gradually broadened over the years to include a wider variety of cases in which penalties were thought to be incommensurate with the gravity of the misdeeds.

Writs were hardly isolated from the way people in general viewed the nature of an orderly (or disorderly) world.

The conditions they dealt with also found expression in literature, not just in the novels of Dickens or Trollope or in Blake's *Songs of Experience* but in newspaper stories and tavern tales. Eventually these voices also found their way into the *corpus juris*, much as the narrative voices of the Harlem Renaissance or the "reality" of Harriet Beecher Stowe's *Uncle Tom's Cabin* crept into the body of American law.

It is not at all clear what it means when changing literary renderings of the world find their way into the *corpus juris*. Common law takes it for granted that established facts become modified by new possibilities, that "God fulfills Himself in many ways, / Lest one good order should corrupt the world." Even landmark legal opinions that convert yesterday's possibility into today's established law are justified on the grounds that nothing has "really" changed.

VII

I have argued that narrative is the medium par exellence for depicting, even caricaturing, human plights, as in "lost child" or "jealous lover" stories or what English common law refers to as *moderata misericordia*. Prototypical plights even become root metaphors of the human condition—like Sisyphus forever pushing his rock uphill, a root metaphor for self-sustaining frustration. Many situations can be assimilated to the image of Sisyphus, even the tenant farmer perpetually in debt to the landlord and forever too poor to buy his plot of land. It is the genius of the Joseph Conrads, the

Italo Calvinos, and the James Joyces to sense the reach of these classic plights and to awaken others to them. And so too great jurists. Eventually our mythic metaphors find their way into the *corpus juris*.

This brings us back to the odd kinship of literary and legal narratives—why Athenians took to the law courts when Aeschylus or Aristophanes was not on the boards, and perhaps even why novelists and playwrights find law courts so irresistible—though they seem contradictory.

Perhaps we should heed the French caution that contradictory stances often have a common border, "*les extrêmes se touchent.*" Literature, exploiting the semblance of reality, looks to the possible, the figurative. Law looks to the actual, the literal, the record of the past. Literature errs toward the fantastic, law toward the banality of the habitual. But each is half a loaf, and in some covert way each knows it. Can we ever fit our discontents in the present to the writs and statutes of the past, as the law would have us do? Or, for that matter, can writers simply imagine the possible worlds they create without brooding over the constraints inherited from their past? How to wed memory and imagination? How does the comfort of predictability come to live with the excitement of possibility? The answer is, of course, that they only do so uneasily, even precariously.

Yet we manage, if sometimes poorly. And so it is with a culture's perpetual narrative dialectic, with the uneasy balance between opposing folk narratives—as when our prototypically American creed of generous opportunity is pitted against our equally American creed of caution: the land of opportunity for all, but don't let the other fellow take advantage of your good nature. Both creeds have found their way into the *corpus juris. Brown* was a striking extension of the creed of opportunity. And however much it has been diluted by new narratives about level playing fields and color-blind justice, it remains a vital force, still open to refreshment and reshaping. But refreshment and reshaping are not products of law's precautionary procedures, not even of its devotion to case precedent, for precedent, too, can become a plaything of the narrative dialectic, as Anthony Amsterdam and I recently sought to demonstrate.[14] A culture's narrative dialectic expresses itself first in the imaginative works of writers and playwrights, and it is virtually impossible to predict whether, when, or how it will express itself in the culture's *corpus juris.* This is so whether in the emperor Justinian's troubled times or in our own. But of one thing we can be certain. It has always mattered that legal pleading and literary storytelling share the medium of narrative, a form that keeps perpetually in play the uneasy alliance between the historically established and the imaginatively possible. Perhaps that's what some legal critics mean by storytelling giving the law back to the people.

I need to turn now to a different arena to explore more fully the broader (and often troubling) question of the dialectic between the comfort of the familiar past and the allure of the possible. In autobiographical narrative that dialectic is forever center stage, and often noisily so.

⚞ THREE ⚟

THE NARRATIVE CREATION
OF SELF

"Self" is a surprisingly quirky idea—intuitively obvious to common sense yet notoriously evasive to definition by the fastidious philosopher. The best we seem to be able to do when asked what it is, is to point a finger at our forehead or our chest. Yet "self" is the common coin of our speech: no conversation goes long without its being unapologetically used. And the legal code simply takes it for granted when it speaks of such legal concepts as responsibility and privacy. We would do well, then, to have a brief look at what the self is, the subject that narrative creation of self is supposed to be about.

Is there some essential self inside that, somehow, is just there? If so, why would we ever need to tell ourselves about ourselves, and why would there be such injunctions as "Know thyself" or "To thine own self be true"? Surely, if our selves were just there, we'd have no need to *tell* ourselves about them. Yet we spend a good deal of time doing just that, either alone, or with friends, or vicariously at the psychiatrist's, or at confession if we are Catholics. What function does such self-telling serve?

The standard twentieth-century answer to this question was that much of our selves was unconscious, created *sub rosa*, and adroitly defended from our conscious probings by various mechanisms that concealed or distorted it. We needed to find ways around these defenses—with the help of a psychoanalyst, in interaction with whom we would reenact the past and overcome our resistance to discovering ourselves. Where there was id, now there shall be ego, to paraphrase Freud. Little question that Freud's solution to our puzzle was a brilliant metaphor and that it had profound effects on our image of self.[1]

Yet we would do well to continue our inquiry. Freud's implied drama of id, ego, and superego, for all its metaphoric brilliance, is unfinished business, and it is to the pursuit of this unfinished business that this chapter is dedicated. The question why we need to tell stories in order to elucidate what we mean by "self" has even come to preoccupy mainstream psychoanalysis.[2]

I want to begin by proposing boldly that, in effect, there is no such thing as an intuitively obvious and essential self to know, one that just sits there ready to be portrayed in words. Rather, we constantly construct and reconstruct our selves to meet the needs of the situations we encounter, and we do so with the guidance of our memories of the past and our hopes and fears for the future.[3] Telling oneself about oneself is like making up a story about who and what we are, what's happened, and why we're doing what we're doing.

It is not that we have to make up these stories from scratch each time. Our self-making stories accumulate over time, even pattern themselves on conventional genres. They get out-of-date, and not just because we grow older or wiser but because our self-making stories need to fit new circumstances, new friends, new enterprises. Our very memories fall victim to our self-making stories. It is not that I can no longer tell you (or myself) the "original, true story" about my desolation in the bleak summer after my father died. Rather, I would be telling you (or myself) a new story about a twelve-year-old "once upon a time." And I could tell it several ways, all of them shaped as much by my life since then as by the circumstances of that long-ago summer.

Self-making is a narrative art, and though it is more constrained by memory than fiction is, it is uneasily constrained, a matter to which we shall come presently. Self-making, anomalously, is from both the inside and the outside. The inside of it, we like to say in our Cartesian way, is memory, feelings, ideas, beliefs, subjectivity. Part of this insidedness is almost certainly innate and species-specific, like our irresistible sense of continuity over time and place and our postural sense of ourselves. But much of self-making is from outside in—based on the apparent esteem of others and on the myriad expectations that we early, even mindlessly, pick up from the culture in which we are immersed.

Besides, narrative acts of self-making are usually guided by unspoken, implicit cultural models of what selfhood should be, might be—and, of course, shouldn't be. Not that we are slaves of culture, as even the most dedicated cultural anthropologists now appreciate.[4] Rather, there are many possible, ambiguous models of selfhood even in simple or ritualized cultures. Yet all cultures provide presuppositions and perspectives about selfhood, rather like plot summaries or homilies for telling oneself or others about oneself.

But these self-making precepts are not rigid commands. They leave ample room for maneuver. Self-making is, after all, our principal means for establishing our uniqueness, and a moment's thought makes plain that we distinguish ourselves from others by comparing our accounts of ourselves with the accounts that others give us of themselves.

Telling others about oneself is, then, no simple matter. It depends on what *we* think *they* think we ought to be like—or what selves in general ought to be like. Nor do our calculations end when we come to telling ourselves about ourselves. Our self-directed self-making narratives early come to express what we think others expect us to be like. Without much awareness of it, we develop a decorum for telling ourselves about ourselves: how to be frank with ourselves, how not to offend others. A thoughtful student of autobiography has proposed that self-narratives (at least written autobiographies) conform to a tacit *pacte autobiographique* governing what constitutes appropriate public self-telling.[5] We follow some variant of it even when we are only telling ourselves about ourselves. In the process, selfhood becomes *res publica*, even when talking to ourselves.

It hardly requires a postmodern leap to conclude, accordingly, that self is also other.[6] Classicists, interestingly, see this phenomenon even in the ancient world. Did not the Roman art of rhetoric, originally designed to aid in arguing convincingly to others, eventually turn inward to self-telling? And might it have produced the resoluteness so characteristic of Roman masculinity?[7] And so the sharp-minded Roman, clear about who and what he was and what was expected of him. Did that self-certainty even shape the emperor Justinian, pushing him at the peak of his career to cleanse all local ambiguity from the administration of Roman law? Is empire affected by the long reach of self-narratives?

Take another example from antiquity, offered by the distinguished Cambridge classicist Sir Geoffrey Lloyd. Lloyd notes, with impressive evidence, that the ancient Greeks were much more confrontational and autonomy-seeking than the then contemporary Chinese.[8] The Greeks, not the Chinese, invented the "winner-takes-all" syllogism for resolving their arguments, while the Chinese, surely as gifted mathematically, avoided such showdown procedures like the plague. Showdowns fit Chinese decorum poorly. Did their method of proof make the Greeks even more confrontational until, as with the rhetoric of the later Romans, it sharpened their sense of their selfhood? Do we invent tools to further our cultural bent and then become their servants, even developing ourselves to fit them?

Americans, it has been said, no longer show as much overt affection as they used to: men worry that it might be taken as sexual harassment if affection is directed toward women, adults worry that it might appear like child abuse if directed toward kids. All of this is the side effect of well-intended prohibitive statutes. A posted notice in one California school district, for example, expressly forbids "showing your affections" (on a list of prohibitions that includes "Don't spit").[9] Will our new guardedness end up obscuring the tender side of our selfhood? Will it become taboo to take account of that tenderness in telling ourselves about ourselves?

I I

Selfhood seems to have become an astonishingly public issue in our times. Endless books tell us how to improve it, how to keep from becoming "divided," narcissistic, isolated, or unsituated. Research psychologists, ordinarily proud of their neutrality, warn us of our "errors" in judging self, that we usually see others as guided by enduring beliefs and dispositions while seeing ourselves as more subtly steered by our circumstances. They call this the primary attribution error.

But hasn't self always been a matter of public, moral concern, even a topic of debate? Self and soul have forever been yin and yang in the Judeo-Christian tradition. Confession of sins and appropriate penance purged the soul—and raised the spirits of one's secular self. Doctrinally, the soul was cursed with original sin, and we know from magisterial works on the history of childhood how important it was considered to purge that sin from selfhood. Calvin's version of original sin was so compelling that it took Rousseau's irony and courage to bid it a bitter farewell in *Émile*.

But the good self has also been an issue in that perpetual cockpit of secular moral debate called pedagogy. Does education make the spirit more generous by broadening the mind? Does selfhood become the richer by exposure to "the best which has been thought and said in the world," in Matthew Arnold's classic phrase? Education was *Bildung*—character building, not just subject matter. Hegel thought he had diagnosed the difficulty: the young (or anybody) had to be inspired to rise above immediate demands by being instructed in the culture's noble history. He went so far as to suggest that pedagogy should "alienate one from the present." Even the allegedly pragmatic John Dewey debated the issue of how to create a self fit for a good society.[10] No generation, it seems, has ever been able to heed the advice of the title of James Thurber's little classic *Let Your Mind Alone!*

One cannot resist the conclusion that the nature and shape of selfhood are indeed as much matters of cultural concern, *res publica*, as of individual concern. Or, to put it another way, selfhood involves a commitment to others as well as being "true to oneself." Selfhood without such commitment constitutes a form of sociopathy—the absence of a sense of responsibility to the requirements of social being. Even so basic a concept in the law as *mens rea*, a guilty mind, and the legal determination of criminal intent would be impossible without this element of social commitment in selfhood.

Small wonder, then, that the self is a public topic and that its "betterment" is regarded not just as a personal matter but as meriting the care of those charged with maintaining a proper moral order—the church, the school, the family, and, of course, the state itself.

We must return to the puzzling question of what self-hood is and how it is fashioned. Let's leave the matter by noting only that self-making and self-telling are about as public activities as any private acts can be. And so are critiques of them.

I I I

Why do we naturally portray ourselves through story, so naturally indeed that selfhood itself seems a product of our own story making? Does the research literature of psychology have any answers? One gifted psychologist, Ulric Neisser, has gathered much of that literature together in several learned volumes containing articles by leading scholars in the field.[11] I've gone back over those volumes with our question in mind—Why narrative?—and let me condense what I found into a dozen "one-liners" about the self:

1. It is teleological and agentive, replete with desires, intentions, and aspirations and endlessly in pursuit of goals.
2. In consequence, it is sensitive to obstacles, real or imagined: responsive to success or failure, unsteady in handling uncertain outcomes.
3. It responds to its judged successes and failures by altering its aspirations and ambitions and changing its reference groups.[12]

4. It relies on selective remembering to adjust the past to the demands of the present and the anticipated future.

5. It is oriented toward "reference groups" and "significant others" who set the cultural standards by which it judges itself.[13]

6. It is possessive and extensible, adopting beliefs, values, loyalties, even objects as aspects of its own identity.

7. Yet it seems able to shed these values and possessions as required by circumstances without losing its continuity.

8. It is experientially continuous over time and circumstances, despite striking transformations in its contents and activities.

9. It is sensitive to where and with whom it finds itself in the world.

10. It is accountable and sometimes responsible for formulating itself in words, becoming troubled when words cannot be found.[14]

11. It is moody, affective, labile, and situation-sensitive.

12. It seeks and guards coherence, eschewing dissonance and contradiction through highly developed psychic procedures.

Not very surprising, hardly counterintuitive in even the smallest detail. It becomes more interesting, though, if you translate it into a set of reminders about how to tell or write a good story. Something like:

1. A story needs a plot.
2. Plots need obstacles to goals.
3. Obstacles make people reconsider.
4. Tell only about the story-relevant past.
5. Give your characters allies and connections.
6. Let your characters grow.
7. But keep their identities intact.
8. And also keep their continuities evident.
9. Locate your characters in the world of people.
10. Let your characters explain themselves as needed.
11. Let your characters have moods.
12. Worry when your characters are not making sense—and have them worry, too.

Should we say, then, that all the psychological research on selfhood was simply a rediscovery of the wheel, that all we've learned from it is that most people learn how to tell passable stories with themselves as the chief protagonists? That would surely be unjust and also plain untrue. But we could certainly fault the psychologists with a failure to tell the dancer from the dance, the medium from the message, or however one puts it. For their "self" comes out to be little more than a standard protagonist in a standard story of a standard genre. She sets out on a quest, runs into obstacles and has second thoughts about her aims in life, remembers what's needed as needed, has allies and people she cares about, yet grows without losing herself in the process. She lives in a recognizable world, speaks her mind when she needs to but is thrown when words fail her, and wonders

whether her life makes sense. It can be tragic, comic, a bildungsroman, whatever. Does selfhood require more than a
reasonably well wrought story, a story whose continuing
episodes tie together (like stories generally, or like lines of
precedent in the law)?

Maybe we're faced with another chicken-and-egg puzzle.
Is our sense of selfhood the *fons et origio* of storytelling, or
does the human gift of narrative endow selfhood with the
shape it takes? But perhaps that oversimplifies. There is an
old adage in linguistics that "thinking is for speaking"—
that we come to think in a certain way in order to say what
we want to say in the language we've learned to use, which
hardly means that *all* thinking is shaped just for the sake of
talking. Dan Slobin, a gifted scholar and a seasoned student
of how language and thought influence each other, puts it
well: "One cannot verbalize experience without taking a
perspective, and . . . the language being used often favors
particular perspectives. The world does not present 'events'
to be encoded in language. Rather, in the process of speaking or writing, experiences are filtered through language
into *verbalized events*."[15] Selfhood can surely be thought of
as one of those "verbalized events," a kind of meta-event
that gives coherence and continuity to the scramble of experience. However, it is not just language per se but narrative
that shapes its use—particularly its use in self-making. Is it
so surprising? Physicists come to think in those equations
they scrawl on blackboards. Musicians are so adept at thinking musically that they need to look at the score as well as
listen to the music to see where something went wrong.
Don't we, too, have to tell the event in order to find out

whether, after all, "this is the kind of person I really mean to be"?

IV

Most people never get around to composing a book-length autobiography. Self-telling is usually provoked by episodes related to some longer-term concern. Though linked to or provoked by particular happenings, it ordinarily presupposes those longer-term, larger-scale concerns—much like history writing, where the *annales*, the records, of particular events are already determined or shaped by a more encompassing *chronique*, which itself bears the stamp of an overarching *histoire*. An account of a battle takes for granted the existence of a war, which takes for granted the larger notions of competitive nation-states and some kind of world order.

No autobiography is completed, only ended. No autobiographer is free from questions about which self his autobiography is about, composed from what perspective, for whom. The one we write is only one *version*, one way of achieving coherence. Autobiography turns even a seasoned writer into a doppelgänger—and turns its readers into sleuths. How can any version of an autobiography strike a balance between what one actually was and what one might have been? We play games with ourselves about this would-be balance. A writer friend and neighbor of mine, a gifted journalist engaged in writing an autobiography, as was I, responded to my doubts with: "No problem for me; I am faithful to memory." Yet she was renowned locally as a delicious fabulist who, in the words of a witty fellow townsman, "could make a shopping trip to Skibbereen sound like a visit to ancient Rome itself." Like her, we are forever balancing what was with what might have been—and, in the main, mercifully unaware of how we do it.

Literary autobiography, for all its pitfalls, has much to teach us about what we leave implicit in more spontaneous, episode-linked, briefer self-accounts. It can even give us hints about the writer's crypto-philosophical notion of what a self is. And that is no idle matter.

A recent book highlights this point vividly—James Olney's thoughtful *Memory and Narrative: The Weave of Life-Writing*.[16] Olney is particularly concerned with the rise and fall of the narrative form in self-accounting and with the question why, in recent times, it has begun losing its allure for literary autobiographers, even if they can't escape it in their more spontaneous and episodic self-telling.

Four famous life writers come under his scrutiny, their work extending over more than a millennium, starting with Saint Augustine, whose *Confessions* virtually pioneered the autobiographical genre in the fourth century, and ending with Samuel Beckett. Augustine sees his search as one for his true life, his true self, and conceives autobiography as a quest for true memory, for reality. For him, one's true life is that which has been given one by God and Providence, and narrative's inherent, unique orderliness reflects the natural form of memory, the form truest to Providence-given being. True memory mirrors the real world, and Augustine accepts that narrative is its medium. His is a narrative realism, and the self that emerges is the gift of revelation, leavened by reason.

Contrast Giambattista Vico in the eighteenth century, next on Olney's historical trajectory. Vico's reflections on the powers of mind led him to cock his eye at Augustine's narrative realism. For him, a life is crafted by the mental acts of those who live it, not by an act of God. Its storylikeness is of our doing, not God's. Vico was perhaps the first radical constructivist, though he was protected by a rationalism that guarded him from the skepticism usually associated with that stance.

Enter Jean-Jacques Rousseau about a half century later, who, alerted by Vico's reflections and emboldened by the new skepticism of his own revolutionary times, raised new doubts about Augustine's stable and innocent narrative realism. Rousseau's *Confessions* are laced with high-spirited skepticism. Yes, acts of mind, not Providence, shape an autobiography, but Rousseau also pokes fun at these acts of mind—their passionate follies and vanity-serving uses. Life stories for Rousseau are more like social games than quests for some higher truth, and that may be one reason he has little patience with notions like original sin. He turns Vico's respect for reason into a rueful and impious skepticism.

Jump ahead two centuries to Samuel Beckett and our own times. Beckett is at one with Vico's reasoned rejection of Augustine's narrative realism and even more in sympathy with Rousseau's wry skepticism. But he explicitly rejects narrative as reflecting the inherent order of life. Indeed, he denies the very notion that there is any inherent order. His is a thoroughgoing fictionalism, his mission to free life writing (as well as literature) from its narrative straitjacket. Life is problematic, not to be shackled in conventional genres. So even his somewhat autobiographical dramas, like *Waiting for Godot*, pose problems rather than answer them. For him, the road is better than the inn: let one be not lulled by the illusion of narrative.

Each—Augustine, Vico, Rousseau, and Beckett—is a child of his historical time, cultivating a fresh image of selfhood and rejecting what was stale. For Augustine, self is the product of revelation-guided narrative, revealing what God had wrought; by the time we reach Beckett, self-told narrative has become a mere *façon d'écrire*, a man-made noose strangling the imagination. But for each of them, the nature and origin of selfhood were issues of deep and debatable concern, and the concern seems not to have diminished, though the issues may have changed drastically. Why did Thomas à Kempis call his account of true monastic selfhood *Imitatio Christi*? Was he pushing Augustinian narrative realism, proposing Christ's depiction of the serving self as the true model? Were the monks and nuns of his times convinced that their selves were trying to be true imitations of Christ's? Reading Thomas with modern eyes, one senses he is like a recruiter glorifying the kind of selfhood that might lure novices into the monastic life or justify staying in it. The contrast implied throughout his stirring little book is with the selfish, secular self. And so it seems with all disquisitions about selfhood. In some indirect way, they are all advertisements for a *right* selfhood, each with its own version of the tempting competition.

And so it is with Virginia Woolf's metaphoric "room of

one's own," her feminist appeal for a change in women's conceptions of their selfhood. Was Jack Kerouac's *On the Road* tuned to reducing the teleological intensity in his generation's style of self-telling and self-making?

One regrets that in Olney's brilliant account of the great innovations in conceptions of selfhood, he did not explore more fully the struggles his heroic authors underwent in their times—Augustine's against blind faith, Vico's against the spirit of the Enlightenment, Rousseau's against an oppressive ancien régime, and Beckett's against literary realism. The four of them obviously shaped new images of selfhood. But like their images, no image of selfhood ever gains a monopoly. We would do well to inquire why this is so. And our inquiry will bring us back to the issues of autonomy and commitment touched on briefly before.

V

A self-making narrative is something of a balancing act. It must, on the one hand, create a conviction of autonomy, that one has a will of one's own, a certain freedom of choice, a degree of possibility. But it must also relate the self to a world of others—to friends and family, to institutions, to the past, to reference groups. But the commitment to others that is implicit in relating oneself to others of course limits our autonomy. We seem virtually unable to live without both, autonomy and commitment, and our lives strive to balance the two. So do the self-narratives we tell ourselves.

Not everyone succeeds. Take one Christopher McCandless, a twenty-three-year-old whose dead body was found several years ago in a deserted bus in the Alaska wilderness. Some autobiographical fragments showed up among his meager possessions, and they tell the story of a "radically autonomous identity gone wrong."[17] "Dealing with things on his own" was his ideal, and he understood Thoreau's injunction "simplify, simplify" to mean that he should depend on nobody, strive for unfettered autonomy. His self-narrative fit this formula: at the end of his days, he was living in remote Alaska, eating only edible plants, and after three months he died of starvation. Shortly before his death, he went to the trouble of taking a self-portrait, the film of which was found in his camera. In it the young man is seated, with one hand raised and holding in the other a block-letter note on which he has written, "I have had a happy life and Thank the Lord. Goodbye and may God Bless All." On a plywood-covered window of the deserted bus that became his last refuge, he scratched this message: "Two Years He walks the Earth . . . Ultimate Freedom. An Extremist. An Aesthetic Voyager Whose Home is *The Road* . . . No Longer To Be Poisoned By Civilization He Flees, And Walks Alone Upon the Land To Become *Lost* in the *Wild*." In the end, even poor Christopher McCandless felt some commitment to others—his commitment offered, mind you, as an act of free will. As he lay alone, starving to death, he still felt impelled to offer God's blessings to those he had spurned, which was an act of grace, a balancing act. Then, perhaps nostalgically, perhaps bitterly, he died. Was he victim or victor in his own story? More than seventy years ago, the great folklorist Vladimir Propp demonstrated how characters and events in folk stories serve as functions in narrative plots: they do not exist on their own. What function did Christopher McCandless's final act play in his story, and how did he tell it to himself?

I once knew a young doctor, disillusioned with the humdrum of private practice, who upon hearing about the organization Médecins sans Frontières began reading its literature and raising money for it at his county medical association meetings. Finally he spent two years doctoring in Africa. On his return, I asked him if he had changed. "Yes," he said, "my life's more all of a piece now." All of a piece? Scattered over two continents? Yes, for now he is not only practicing medicine back where he'd started but researching the roiling history of the town he'd left to go off to Africa, the better to find the sources of his discontent, to reconcile his autonomy with his commitment to a town which he is making part of the wider world he had longed for. In doing so, he has created a viable self. He's even enlisted the town fathers as his allies in the effort!

How indeed does one balance autonomy and commitment in one's sense of self, let alone make it all of a piece? I had studied that question as a psychologist in the usual indirect way we psychologists do and dutifully contributed my chapter to one of those Neisser volumes I mentioned earlier. But somehow the balance comes out more plainly in ordinary conversation. So I've been asking people about it casually when the topic seems right—friends, people with whom I work, acquaintances. I simply ask them outright about themselves whenever the topic of balancing seems natural. One was a law student, a young woman who was deeply committed to child advocacy in support of parents during child-related litigation. I asked her how she got into that work, which seemed to suit her to a T. She said she'd send me an e-mail, and here is what it said:

It was in some ways inadvertent. I had graduated with a B.A. in English and creative writing, and didn't want to go into education or publishing, etc., but did want to do something . . . to better the lives of poor children. By a peculiar turn of circumstances I fell into an internship with the Community Legal Aid Society in a middle-sized city in the East, where I worked closely with an attorney who was representing parents (often with mental disabilities) in abuse and neglect cases. I was immediately drawn to the work. Most of all, I was astounded by the strength of these parents in the face of tremendous environmental adversity, but also by the way their voices were heard by no one. When they encountered someone (the attorney I worked with, myself) who was truly interested in listening to them, they often weren't able to trust the relationship, and this in turn interfered with effective legal representation. Having done a lot of my own work to "find my voice" and to learn firsthand the healing, even transformative power of being in a relationship with someone who really listened, I felt very connected to these parents, despite our differences in background, etc. So, in the end, it is a continuation of my very deep, very personal interest. . . .

Both the doctor and the child advocate had reached impasses: bored and discontented, going on and on with foreseeable duties to fulfill established commitments. Medical school, then internship, then small-town private practice. The well-brought-up daughter of literary bent, on to college and on to teaching high-school English. Both were following trajectories shaped early in life by conventional commitment. Neither was in material need; they did not have to continue. Both foresaw the next step too clearly, as if possibility had been closed off by the sheer predictability of what lay ahead.

Commitment under these conditions is a narrative that is reminiscent of the law stories discussed in Chapter 2. It is dominated by precedent-obligations in one's own life. Medical graduates go on to internships and then into practice—with small-town practice perhaps being an off-the-track fillip. Circumstances change. The balancing act between commitment and autonomy no longer satisfies as the range of possibilities narrows. One's self-narrative seems lacking in those possible worlds that imagination generates and that novelists and dramatists cultivate.

We can think of these times in life in several ways that are now familiar to us from earlier chapters. We can think of them as akin to the times at which circumstances are ripe for a landmark decision by a court of law. And like landmark decisions, where an earlier doctrinal principle is expanded to take account of new conditions, turning points in life honor old aspirations in new ways. Medical care is not just for the safe and the hometown familiars but also for the deprived and beleaguered beyond a horizon one had not realized existed. Or one gives one's more developed voice to those who need it in their defense, not just to those who would routinely find it on their own. Or poor Christopher McCandless: if self-sufficiency is good, then let it be total. Or one can conceive turning points in one's self-telling as like a self-generated peripeteia, one's previously coping with trouble having now generated trouble of its own.

The bald fact of the matter is that one rarely encounters autobiographies, whether written or spontaneously told in interview, that are without turning points. And they are almost always accompanied by remarks such as "I became a new woman," or "I found a new voice," or "It was a new me after I walked out." Are these an integral part of growing up—like the Sturm und Drang of adolescence? Perhaps, though they certainly are not a feature only of youth, for turning points often occur later in life, particularly as retirement approaches. It may well be that Erik Erikson's renowned "life stages," marked by a shift in concern from autonomy to competence to intimacy to continuity, set the stage for autobiographical turning points.

Some cultures provide for them ritually, as *rites de passage*, and they are often sufficiently painful or taxing to get the idea across. A !Kung Bushman boy is put through a painful ceremonial (which includes having ashes rubbed into fresh cuts in his cheeks, tomorrow's proud scars of manhood) designed to mark his passage out of childhood. Now he is fit to be a hunter, ready to reject a child's ways. He's taken on a hunt soon after, and much hoopla is made about his role in killing a giraffe or whatever gets snagged. The rite of passage not only encourages but legitimates change.[18]

It is not only in *rites de passage* (or in Erikson's life stages) that turning points are conventionalized. Self-narrating, if I may state it again, is from the outside in as well as from the inside out. When circumstances ready us for change, we turn to others who have lived through one, become open to new trends and new ways of looking at ourselves in the world. We read novels with new interest, go to political demonstrations, listen with a more open ear. Lawyers bored with the routines of mergers and copyright-infringement suits pay new attention to what the American Civil Liberties Union is up to. A rising and discontented Jane Fonda, on her own testimony, begins reading the "new" feminist literature to help her understand a divorce through which she has just gone. And, indeed, feminism offers changing versions of a woman's selfhood: from feminine consciousness in a Willa Cather or a Katherine Mansfield, to the protest feminism of a Simone de Beauvoir or a Germaine Greer, to today's activist "equality" feminists.

Self-making through self-narrating is restless and endless, probably more so now than ever before. It is a dialectical process, a balancing act. And despite self-assuring homilies about people never changing, they do. They rebalance their autonomy and their commitments, usually in a way that honors what they were before. Decorum keeps most of us from the sorts of wild adventure in self-making that brought Christopher McCandless down.

V I

What is there to say in conclusion about the narrative art of self-making?

Sigmund Freud in an interesting book too seldom read remarked that each of us is like an entire cast of characters in a novel or play.[19] Novelists and playwrights, he wrote, construct their works of art by splitting up their interior cast of characters, putting them on the page or onstage to work out their relations with each other. Those characters can be heard in the pages of any autobiography. Perhaps it is a literary exaggeration to call our multiple inner voices characters. But they are there to be heard, trying to come to terms with each other, sometimes at loggerheads. An extensive self-making narrative will try to speak for them all, but we know already that no single story can do that. To whom are you telling it, and to what end? Besides, we are too Hamlet-like to make it all of a piece—too torn between the familiar and the possible.

None of this seems to discourage us. We go on, constructing ourselves through narrative. Why is narrative so essential, why do we need it for self-definition? The narrative gift seems to be our natural way of using language for characterizing those deviations from the expected state of things that characterize living in a human culture. None of us knows the just-so evolutionary story of its rise and survival. But what we do know is that it is irresistible as a way of making sense of human interaction.

I have argued that it is through narrative that we create and re-create selfhood, that self is a product of our telling and not some essence to be delved for in the recesses of subjectivity. There is now evidence that if we lacked the capacity to make stories about ourselves, there would be no such thing as selfhood. Let me offer this evidence.

A neurological disorder called dysnarrativia, a severe impairment in the ability to tell or understand stories, is associated with neuropathies like Korsakov's syndrome and Alzheimer's disease.[20] It is more than an impairment of memory about the past, which is itself highly disruptive of one's sense of self, as Oliver Sacks's work has made plain.[21] In Korsakov's syndrome particularly, where affect as well as memory is severely impaired, selfhood virtually vanishes. Sacks describes one of his severe Korsakov patients as "scooped out, de-souled."[22]

One characteristic symptom in such cases is an almost complete loss of the ability to read other minds, to tell what others might have been thinking, feeling, even seeing. Sufferers seem to have lost not only a sense of self but also a sense of other. An astute critic of autobiography, Paul John Eakin, commenting on this literature, takes this evidence as further proof that selfhood is profoundly relational, that self, as noted earlier, is also other.

The emerging view is that dysnarrativia is deadly for selfhood. Eakin cites the conclusion of an unpublished paper by Kay Young and Jeffrey Saver: "Individuals who have lost the ability to construct narratives have lost their selves."[23] The construction of selfhood, it seems, cannot proceed without a capacity to narrate.

Once we are equipped with that capacity, we can produce a selfhood that joins us with others, that permits us to hark back selectively to our past while shaping ourselves for the possibilities of an imagined future. We gain the self-told narratives that make and remake our selves from the culture in which we live. However much we may rely on a functioning brain to achieve our selfhood, we are virtually from the start expressions of the culture that nurtures us. And culture itself is a dialectic, replete with alternative narratives about what self is or might be. The stories we tell to create ourselves reflect that dialectic.

✦ FOUR ✦

SO WHY NARRATIVE?

One truth is surely self-evident: for all that narrative is one of our evident delights, it is serious business. For better or worse, it is our preferred, perhaps even our obligatory medium for expressing human aspirations and their vicissitudes, our own and those of others. Our stories also impose a structure, a compelling reality on what we experience, even a philosophical stance. By their very nature, stories take for granted that their protagonists are free unless ensnared by circumstances. They also take for granted that people know what the world is like, what can be expected of it, as well as what is expected of them. In time, life comes not so much to imitate art as to join with it. It is "ordinary people doing ordinary things in ordinary places for ordinary reasons." A seeming breach in this ordinariness is required to trigger the rich dynamic of narrative—how to cope with it, to domesticate it, to get things back on a familiar track.

Narrative is profoundly a folk art, trading in common beliefs about what people are like and what their world is like. It specializes in what is in jeopardy, or what is presumed to be in jeopardy. Story making is our medium for coming to terms with the surprises and oddities of the human condition and for coming to terms with our imperfect grasp of that condition. Stories render the unexpected less surprising, less uncanny: they domesticate unexpectedness, give it a sheen of ordinariness. "That's odd, that story, but it makes sense, doesn't it," we say often, even when reading Mary Shelley's *Frankenstein*.

Domestication is a major means for maintaining a culture's coherence. Culture, after all, prescribes our notions of ordinariness. But given human unruliness and the imperfections of social control, the expected does not always prevail. We cheat, we seduce, we fail to live up to our pledges. Breaches and aberrations may not be welcome, but they are hardly unexpected. The human condition in the small is too uncertain, and the will too impulsive—on that particular afternoon. So stories are about things in the small. They claim no explicit moral generality, only imply it—until a lawyer gets hold of it to show that by precedent it is in violation of Article IV, Section 3 of some statutory code, which may be why so many clients find the legal process unbearable.

Breaches of the ordinary, once domesticated in narrative, bear the stamp of the culture, not a seal of approval from *Good Housekeeping* but one in the form of "Oh, *that* old story again." Once dignified as a genre or as old hat, they become legitimized as interpretable transgressions or mishaps or lapses in human judgment—the ungrateful child, the faithless spouse, the thieving servant. They become the stock unexpected, and we let ourselves be comforted into believing that there is nothing new under the sun. Breaches become *our* breaches, the Catholic's list of cardinal and venial sins, the Englishman's writs from the King's Bench, the familiarly forbidden.

But as I've commented before, culture is not all of a piece, and neither are its stock stories. Its vitality lies in its dialectic, in its need to come to terms with contending views, clashing narratives. We hear many stories and take them as stock even when they conflict with each other. We understand Creon's bitter refusal to let his treasonable nephew Polynices be buried, but we also understand Antigone's trying to bury her dead brother in defiance of Creon. The vengeful monarch and the loyal sister are at loggerheads. How is it resolved? Then another stock narrative puts the conflict more comfortably in place: both Antigone and Polynices are children of that tragic union of Oedipus and his mother, Jocasta. What can follow but disaster? Creon condemns Antigone to death: political order must prevail. And in swift order, Creon's wife and his own son, Antigone's betrothed, kill themselves in grief and mortification. It was the genius of Sophocles to turn a chilling plight into an "understandable inevitability."

We are still gripped by *Antigone* more than two millennia later, forever bringing it up to date. Jean Anouilh's version of it opened in Paris in the last year of the German occupation, with King Creon a caricature of a modern dictator and Antigone a thinly veiled Marianne/Jeanne d'Arc. So compelling, so ancient is *Antigone*'s dilemma that the Nazi occupiers dared not ban it for fear of mockery. All Paris flocked to the theater, with not even standing room to be had. As a personal aside, I can report that our underground Maquis contacts in Paris sent ironic messages to us in London about weeping German officers in the audience. But I, too, wept my way through the play some months later, when our psychological-warfare unit finally reached liberated Paris, though my tears doubtless had a somewhat different salt. The play went on for another year!

Great dramatic works, like foundational myths, are not models to be copied but awesome breaches in ordinariness to be comprehended, somehow to be domesticated, incorporated in a cultural tradition. Copy the Prince of Denmark, or Agamemnon, or the young captain in Conrad's "The Secret Sharer"? Poor McCandless, copying *Walden* to his lonely death! Great drama and storytelling, in contrast to mere entertainment, serve a perilous function, and we are now far enough along in our account to consider this matter more closely.

Human culture, *any* human culture, is in its nature both a solution to communal living and, more covertly, a threat and challenge to those who live within its bounds. If a culture is to survive, it needs means for dealing with the conflicts of interest inherent in communal living. Systems of exchange (to use Lévi-Strauss's old expression) are one means: my services for your goods or your respect or whatever. "Serious play" (to borrow Clifford Geertz's inspired expression) is another: ways of working out and displacing poisoning conflicts of aspirations in elaborate ritual, as in the famous Javanese cockfight Geertz so vividly chronicled.

Or, all else failing, we devise a legal system and give everybody, presumably, a day in court.

No human culture can operate without some means of dealing with either the foreseeable or the unforeseeable imbalances inherent in communal living. Whatever else it may do, culture must devise means for containing incompatible interests and aspirations. A culture's narrative resources— its folktales, its old-hat stories, its evolving literature, even its modes of gossip—conventionalize the inequities it generates and thereby contain its imbalances and incompatibilities.

I I

Through narrative, we construct, reconstruct, in some ways reinvent yesterday and tomorrow. Memory and imagination fuse in the process. Even when we create the possible worlds of fiction, we do not desert the familiar but subjunctivize it into what might have been and what might be. The human mind, however cultivated its memory or refined its recording systems, can never fully and faithfully recapture the past, but neither can it escape from it. Memory and imagination supply and consume each other's wares.

The law is intriguing because it aspires to look to the past and to memory to determine whether or not a present case story is an exemplar, a recurrence, of what had been proscribed or permitted in the past. But the culture's evolving dialectic usually saves it from falling victim to this impossible mnemonic ideal. Yesterday's separate but equal

becomes today's oppression. And even the past is redefined
—as when the justices in *Brown* cited with approval a 1772
ruling of the King's Bench in *Somerset's Case* declaring that
an escaped black slave who had been transported from the
colonies to England by his master could not be forced back
into bondage on English soil, on grounds that there were no
"municipal statutes" in the country expressly authorizing
slavery, that man's natural state was freedom. One cannot
help admiring this citation in Chief Justice Earl Warren's
historic *Brown* opinion. I admire even more his imaginative
insight in seeing its kinship to the issue of whether or not
separate-but-equal schools violated the equal-protection
clause of the United States Constitution, a document
drafted seventeen years after Lord Mansfield, the lord high
chancellor, set Somerset free.

Narrative fiction creates possible worlds—but they are
worlds extrapolated from the world we know, however much
they may soar beyond it. The art of the possible is a perilous
art. It must take heed of life as we know it, yet alienate us
from it sufficiently to tempt us into thinking of alternatives
beyond it. It challenges as it comforts. In the end, it has the
power to change our habits of conceiving what is real, what
canonical. It can even undermine the law's dictates about
what constitutes a canonical reality. *The Grapes of Wrath*
changed the legitimacy of a neglected American dust bowl
just as surely as *Uncle Tom's Cabin* undermined the accept-
ability of slavery—and not only by stirring popular indigna-
tion. John Steinbeck's novel, like Harriet Beecher Stowe's,
opened the issue of whether life had to be that way. That is
the seed of subversion.

III

What of the balance between memory and imagination in self-making narratives—some conclusion about which should now properly concern us? Before I offer one, I need first to speculate about the origins, the prehistory of story-telling, the better to understand how its different forms relate to each other. Alas, I shall have to do so on fragile evidence, for we will probably never have a reliable record of the earliest spoken stories. Nonetheless, a gifted anthropologist, Victor Turner, offers some interesting conjectures about how the journey started. He sees narrative's beginnings in the communal rituals of early man—in rites of planting, harvest, curing, whatever. Evidence drawn from contemporary nonliterate cultures suggests that everybody participates in these rituals, reenacting events in a manner to bring good fortune. In time, Turner speculates, the performance of rituals was given over to priests, with other tribesmen as their reverent audience.[1] The emergence of priests and shamans as the performers of ritual is, for Turner, the seed from which theater eventually grew.

How does one get from priest-enacted ritual before a tribal audience to theater? Might some gifted shaman or priest have entranced viewers with his thespian brilliance? A great performance with neighboring tribesmen invited to behold it? But though that may have been a step from mere ritual to theater, there would still be a long way to go. How did secular drama or tale-telling come into being?

Paleoarchaeology has some hints. We know that roughly a million years ago there was an enormous increase in the brain size of our ancestral hominids. Merlin Donald, a neuroscientist and distinguished student of man's hominid prehistory, suggests that the increase led not only to an improvement in hominid intelligence but, more specifically, to the emergence of a human "mimetic sense," a form of intelligence that enabled our ancestors to reenact or imitate events in the present or past.[2] As Donald notes, imitation (or mimesis) offers untold advantages in passing on a culture's ways. Let me add as an aside that *Homo sapiens* is the only truly imitative-emulative species in the animal kingdom, despite monkey-see-monkey-do folktales.[3]

How do we get from mimesis to storytelling or playacting, both of which require language, about whose origins and early uses we know virtually nothing? We needn't cower in our ignorance—like the timid program committee of the Académie Française that in the late nineteenth century banned all reports on the prehistory of language from its meetings. Let me offer a few conjectures based on what we know about language now.

One of language's most powerful and universal design features is its so-called remoteness of reference—the power of linguistic expressions to refer to things not in the here and now of either speaker or listener. This takes language beyond mere pointing, or "ostension." A second design feature, also universal, is arbitrariness of reference, which has the effect of freeing us from the more binding restrictions of pure mimesis: signs do not have to resemble their referents, as they do in representational painting. The little monosyllable "whale" stands for a huge creature, while the bulky polysyllable "microorganism" stands for a speck of a one. As with remoteness, we take arbitrariness for granted. These are two of the most important features of human speech. Add one other universal feature of language mentioned in Chapter 1 in connection with Emmy's monologues: case grammar, so-called—a syntax that distinguishes agent, action, recipient of action, instrument of action, setting, and direction and progress of action. Different languages do it differently—by prefix or suffix, by position in a sentence, whatever. But they all do it, all make these distinctions.

The three together—remoteness, arbitrariness, and case grammar—equip us to talk of things not present, to do so without reenacting their scale or shape, and to mark the flow of human, ongoing action. The ritual actor-priest can wish the new planting well in words, and so too the chronicler recounting a clash with neighboring tribesmen or the father telling his son about exemplary ancestors. And these stories can be told anywhere, by the fireside, years later, to one at a time or many, even just to oneself. The tools are there for narrative, and given that storytelling appears very early in children, might we not speculate that it appeared very early among the talking hominids—that ontogeny recapitulates phylogeny, that if little kids understand story almost as soon as they grasp remoteness and arbitrariness and some primitive case grammar, maybe early *Homo sapiens* did?

Our knowledge of archaic folklore, thanks to Vladimir Propp's and Albert Lord's pioneering work, suggests one other thing about early stories: they were a staple in marking special occasions and, on such occasions, were told by recognized storytellers—the "singers of tales," as Lord called them in his celebrated book of 1960.[4] Skill in storytelling is recognized and honored in even the simplest societies. And the skill has a formal structure that goes beyond mere expressiveness. Folklore studies offer ample evidence that stories told by the teller of tales were composed of strings of module-like hunks that could be re-strung to generate different tales for different occasions. Would it have taken long for genres of narrative to spring up? And for geniuses in their composition to emerge? There would have been plenty of inducement for a Homer to exhibit his gifts, and tellers of tales are among the tribe's most honored members.

Would life not have begun imitating art before long? Could human beings ever resist emulating the acts and styles of the artfully told stories offered by the tellers of tales? Did the Greeks believe in their myths? as the classicist Paul Veyne has asked. Well, yes and no. But as another great scholar, E. R. Dodds, put it, they certainly took heed of those myths in how they lived their lives and experienced their world.[5]

Alas, we shall never know about the more intimate tale-telling of our ancestors—*en famille*, out hunting or gathering edible shrubs, at leisure (and all societies ever studied have considerable leisure time). But again, we can make some informed guesses. Let me frame it in terms made familiar by the great Russian psychologist Lev Vygotsky.[6] He uses the expression "internalization" to characterize how we take over and emulate established ways of talking and telling, and then make them our own. He, along with his gifted student Alexander Luria, offers stunning examples of internalization at work among simple Kazakh peasants first coming into contact with mechanized collective farming in the early years of the Russian Revolution. Not only did their ideas about nature change, even what makes the clouds move, but so did their ideas about themselves, who they were and what they had or didn't have within their power to accomplish. The social world changed for them, and so did their selves.

IV

Come back now to self-making as the product of self-telling. Granting that we're endowed at the outset with some primitive, innate capacity for creating a kind of wordless spatiotemporal and postural self-continuity from the inside, as it were, much of the rest of self-making is from the outside, affected by our interaction with others. Not that there aren't crucial and even lonely moments of self-reflection, even early on, when the young child tries to balance autonomy and connection while achieving separation from her mother or gaining control of her own attention. These matters have been given close scrutiny by researchers on infancy and childhood in recent decades.[7] And they merit it, for they are the opening chapters in a lifelong story of how we struggle to strike a balance between autonomy and connectedness— the failure of which finally struck down Christopher Mc-Candless.

But it would be mistaken to see this struggle as a forever-fluid cavalry encounter. In time it becomes more like trench warfare. We create our self-defining stories to meet the situations where we will go on living. We become family members with family stories. We remain members of the Class of 1962 at Harvard or of our class at Shady Hill ten years earlier. We nourish our identities by our connections yet insist that we are something more as well—ourselves. And that unique identity derives in major part from the stories we tell ourselves to put those fragmentary pieces together. Like the Greeks listening to Homer, we are drawn to the mythic designs of our times. We may not quite believe in them (as Paul Veyne tells us the Greeks didn't quite believe in theirs), but we take them into account in the pattern of our lives. And when they fit new circumstances poorly, we domesticate the bad fit with stories like those that make it "reasonable" for Creon and Antigone to have got into such a mess over the burial of Polynices.

We are, as Claude Lévi-Strauss remarks, *bricoleurs*, improvisers. We improvise in how we tell about ourselves to ourselves, improvise in the interest of keeping our investment in our balance from getting undone. And here too we are beneficiaries of the culture's ongoing dialectic. For we have a stock of stories, old stories, to draw on for representing our imbalances to ourselves. When in doubt, we can even fall back on the old saw about being basically all right though in a bad patch. Just as our opposable forefingers and thumbs enable us to use many tools, our narrative gift gives us access to the culture's treasury of stories. And if we can't manage it alone, there are institutional resources to fall back on: the priest, the psychoanalyst, the self-help shelf.

SO WHY NARRATIVE?

V

When I was a zealous young psychologist eager to encompass the world, I wrote a little book called *On Knowing: Essays for the Left Hand.* It was intended to celebrate how imagination's artful intuitions about the human condition gave us a running start into understanding that same human condition in a more sobersided "scientific" way. The left hand of intuition offered riches to the right hand of reason.

It is a book preoccupied with how narratives of the imagination could be transformed into ones that could be tested, proven, verified—science. The scientific method, I believed then, could tame ordinary narrative into testable hypotheses and test them.

I think now that my youthful and yearning belief that there were two mutually translatable worlds of mind, the paradigmatic and the narrative, was profoundly mistaken. Yes, a paradigmatic mode of thought relies on the verification of well-formed propositions about how things are. And yes, the narrative one is also directed toward the world, not toward how things are but toward how things might be or might have been. The paradigmatic mode is existential and declarative: there is an x of property y such that its orbit has the property z. The narrative one is normative and its mode subjunctive: Creon should have let Polynices be buried, and his refusal to do so brought unfathomable disaster on everyone, including those he most loved. How can we translate from one world of mind to the other?

Could we, in the spirit of the paradigmatic one, offer the

101

hypothesis that if Agamemnon had "explained" to his wife, Clytemnestra, why, in honor, he had to obey the oracle and sacrifice their daughter Iphigenia to obtain fair winds for the fleet to depart for Troy, then all would have gone well between them? An eager young social psychologist might then devise an appropriate experiment to test the hypothesis. How? A controlled laboratory situation—but to test what? Couples where the husband tries to explain to his wife why he had to spend the family savings to bail out his brother's business? Is that what the story of Agamemnon, Clytemnestra, and Iphigenia is about? "You've forgotten the curse on the house of Atreus? You don't understand." And the eager young social psychologist would say, "But it is you who don't understand. I was testing the placatory value of full explanations of husbands to wives."

Sophocles and Aeschylus were virtuously occupied, writing their plays about the fateful house of Atreus. And so too our young social psychologist, doing her clever experiment. If her experiment bears fruit, perhaps it will help us guide married couples toward richer, less contentious lives. But the gift of playwrights is something else: they have given us a treasury of metaphor about tragic plights, images of the possible in an imperfect world.

Surely we can live with the two, the austere but well-defined world of the paradigmatic and the darkly challenging world of narrative. Indeed, it is when we lose sight of the two in league that our lives narrow. I have always been moved by the anthropology done some years ago by a friend of mine, Shirley Brice Heath. She studied how kids came by their "ways with words," comparing lower-class black children in Trackton with middle-class white ones in Roadville (pseudonyms of two nearby towns in North Carolina). The black kids received praise locally for imaginatively elaborated tales of their daily doings, and they got better and better at it. But the white kids were enjoined by parents and teachers alike to "stick to the facts"—and they, too, got better at it.[8]

Doubtless the kids in Roadville and Trackton eventually came to their own conclusions about how the *real* world *really* is—and doubtless they were more fanciful in Trackton than in Roadville. Van Orman Quine, as delightful an ironist as he was towering as a philosopher, was fond of teasing hard-line realists with what he called "the philosopher's version" of Haeckel's theorem about ontogeny recapitulating phylogeny, about the course of embryological growth mirroring the evolutionary development of the species. The Quinean version was that "ontology recapitulates epistemology," that our notions of what is real are made to fit our ideas about how we come to know "reality." I'm suggesting that what stories do is like that: we come to conceive of a "real world" in a manner that fits the stories we tell about it, but it is our good philosophical fortune that we are forever tempted to tell different stories about the presumably same events in the presumably real world. The tyranny of the single story surely led our forebears to guarantee freedom of expression, as in the First Amendment to the United States Constitution. Let many stories bloom.

Yet, despite such guarantees, the stereotyped single story still imposes an ontological hardening on our various versions of the real world. An end-of-the-century sobersided investigation by two psychologists provides a striking demonstration. How are purportedly true news stories about American youth told in the mass media, and what version of "reality" do they create in those exposed to them? Our two conscientious investigators brought to bear the full tool kit of research techniques: content analyses of the media, opinion surveys, open-ended interviews, focus groups, metaphor analyses, the lot. And, to boot, they surveyed the related research literature on this subject with a thoroughness that few other than social scientists ever bring to such an enterprise.[9]

Here are some examples of their findings. The mass media have few enough stories to tell about youth, in general or about particular ones. Only about one in twenty-five news stories on the television networks mentions young people, and even on local news they show up in only one in twelve. The three most frequent sorts of youth stories concern crime victimization, accidents involving the young, or violent juvenile crime, which together make up about half of the news stories reported. Not surprisingly, fewer than two in ten adult Americans believe that young people share their moral and ethical values. Parents of teenagers are much less prone to be taken in by media stereotypes of the young, again not surprisingly, but they're still susceptible in an indirect way: they take their own teenagers as "exceptional" and seem willing to accept media stereotypes of American youth in general. Yet there's one encouraging finding: adults who feel well disposed to the young (despite the media) often justify their positive views by pointing to group sports, to the performing arts, or to community/

volunteer service done by kids. But, alas, news stories rarely deal with these.

Let me end with two cautionary tales of what happens when we isolate narrative and bare factuality from each other. Both tales concern life-and-death matters, and, as it happens, both have to do with the practice of medicine—one with routine hospital procedures, the other with occupational therapy and rehabilitation for victims of road accidents and other hazards of contemporary life.

The distinguished College of Physicians and Surgeons, Columbia University's School of Medicine in New York, has a newly formed Program in Narrative Medicine that concerns itself with what has come to be called narrative ethics. It was set up in response to the increasing realization of the suffering—even deaths—attributable in part or in whole to doctors having ignored what patients told them about their illnesses, what they had to cope with, their sense of being neglected, even deserted. It is not that the doctors did not keep track of the cases, for they faithfully followed their patients' charts—heart rate, blood counts, temperature, and the results of specialized tests. But, to paraphrase one of the physicians working in this program, they simply didn't listen to what the patients told them, to the patients' stories. In their view, they were doctors "sticking to the facts."

In consequence, some patients gave up hope, quit the fight for life. In fact—and that is surely the right expression—patients' stories often contained the very hints that should have warned attending physicians that a course of treatment was not working. In one published case, the stories might have warned them that a debilitating depres-

sion was setting in that would vitiate the effects of the pre-
scribed medications. "A life," to quote the same physician,
"is not a record on a chart." If a patient is expecting a quick,
big effect from some intervention or medication and none is
forthcoming, the slide downhill has a biological side as well
as a psychic one.

What is narrative medicine? I asked. Your responsibility
is to listen to what the patient has to say, and then figure out
what to do about it. After all, who owns his life, you or he?
Not irrelevantly, the doctor I have been quoting, Rita
Charon, not only is a respected physician but holds a doctor-
ate in literature for a dissertation on Henry James![10] More to
the point, the program has already begun reducing deaths
due to narrative incompetencies at P&S.

A similar story comes from the Occupational Science De-
partment at the University of Southern California's School
of Medicine. The program there was set in motion by pioneering studies carried out by the anthropologist Cheryl
Mattingly, now on the USC School of Medicine staff. An anthropologist in a medical school is not new. There has long
been an anthropological specialty devoted to the practice of
healing in different cultures of the world. But only in recent
decades have anthropologists become involved with the
practice of medicine at home.

The project in question has to do with how to get gravely
injured children or children recovering from disabling illnesses into function-restoring, sometimes lifesaving "occupational" therapy. The USC group has been at this work
long enough to have reached one very large and very reliable conclusion: it is not enough to design the right exer-

cises, not enough to have a competent physical therapist to administer them, not enough to convince the parent that the exercise regimen is crucial to restoration of function. There must also be a narrative of possible recovery, even a fanciful one that casts the child-patient, the therapist, and a parent in a Wild West story or a detective drama. Never mind that the story has to do figuratively with rounding up cattle, a few more each day, or that you're yanking your way back to school a step at a time literally. A shared narrative is what matters. Reason alone does not turn the trick. The exercises that kids must do are always uncomfortable, often painful. Never mind that the doctor assures you that "regular exercise will make you well, young fellow."[11]

Narrative, we are finally coming to realize, is indeed serious business—whether in law, in literature, or in life. Serious, yes, and something else as well. There is surely no other use of mind that gives such delights while at the same time posing such perils.

NOTES

ONE: THE USES OF STORY

1. A pocket history of our subject might be of some help at the outset. There is an ancient though sparse literature on the nature, uses, and mastery of narrative that begins seriously with Aristotle's *Poetics*. His concern was principally with the manner in which literary forms "imitated" life—the issue of mimesis. Medieval scholarship was never centrally occupied with this question, and the burgeoning rationalism of the Renaissance and the Enlightenment pushed the study of narrative into the background; we shall visit some pre-Renaissance views on the matter in Chapter 3.

It was perhaps Vladimir Propp who, in Russia just after the revolution, brought concern with narrative back to life. Propp was a folklorist strongly influenced by the new formalism of Russian linguistics, though he was enough of a humanist to recognize that the structure of the story form not only was a matter of syntax but also reflected the human effort to cope with the untoward and unexpected in life. He was in search of the universal plights depicted in the world's folklore, in much the same spirit as linguists of his time were in search of purely grammatical universals. His work achieved a *succès d'estime* in postrevolutionary Russia, and his fame spread to the English-speaking world when his *Morphology of the Folktale* (Austin: University of Texas Press, 1968) was translated into English. Yet in that book as well as in his later *Theory and History of Folklore* (Minneapolis: University of Minnesota Press, 1984), his preoccupation with the structural universals of folkloric plights kept him from exploring the varied uses beyond mere storytelling to which narrative is put. Still, Propp deserves full credit for having launched the modern study of narrative.

The literary critic and polymath Kenneth Burke revived Aristotle's thinking in his brilliant volume *A Grammar of Motives* (New York: Prentice-Hall, 1945). His consuming interest was in the necessary conditions for the portrayal of drama, and he considered narrative "dramatism" a reflection of our artfulness in coping with human trouble. Indeed, Burke's morphology of human Trouble (his capital *T*, not mine) still stands as a guide for students of narrative.

But Burke was bucking the formalist tide of his times. Structuralism continued to ride high in the postwar years. The anthropologist Claude Lévi-Strauss, for example, adapted Propp's emphasis on invariant story sequences to fit his own claim that folktales and myths mirrored the contrastive and conflicted binary structures of the cultures in which they came into being, as in the elementary contrastive pair in the title of one of his key books, *The Raw and the Cooked* (New York: Harper & Row, 1969), the contrast here standing for the primitive opposition between nature and culture. For Lévi-Strauss, myth and story were manifestations of a culture's coming to terms with the conflicting requirements of communal living. Narrative reflected a culture's inherent strains in effecting the kinds of exchange required in communal life.

The 1960s—the birth years of Noam Chomsky's linguistics, of the cognitive revolution, of artificial intelligence—were not great years for narrative studies in the human sciences. Story and its forms were left to the literary community and to a few historians. But there were exceptions, for linguists have always been beguiled by poetics, and the story form is a classic topic in poetics. Indeed, a distinguished linguist of that period, William Labov, published a classic article on the subject (William Labov and Joshua Waletzky, "Narrative Analysis," in *Essays on the Verbal and Visual Arts*, Proceedings of the 1966 annual spring meeting of the American Ethnological Society, ed. June Helm [Seattle: University of Washington Press, 1967]). Labov was principally interested in the language of narrative, but he was also concerned with the uses to which narrative is put. Like Aristotle, he saw narrative as our means of making sense of, coming to terms with the unexpected, the untoward. Perhaps it is a sign of a renewal of concern with narrative that this 1960s classic has recently been republished with commentaries (including one by me) as a whole issue of the *Journal of Narrative and Life History* 7 (1997): 3–38.

Interest in narrative has grown steadily in the last decade or two, particularly in the power of the story form to shape our conceptions of reality and legitimacy. There has indeed been a "narrative turn," with historians often leading the way, in revolt against depersonalized sociological and Marxist renderings of the past. In the English-speaking world, the call for a return to narrative history came from scholars like Hayden White, Simon Schama, and Arthur Danto; in France, from historians of the *Annales* school like Georges Duby and François Furet. But the narrative turn affected many other fields as well. Was it disenchantment with cut-and-dried, impersonal history, sociology, and anthropology that produced it? Or was it a response to the enormous personal suffering and dislocation of the most destructive century in human history?

The study of autobiography also took the turn—autobiography not just as a depiction of an era's representative lives but as an expression of the human condition under particular historical circumstances. Soon to be well known literary critics like William Spengemann and James Olney in America and Philippe Lejeune in France began to explore life writing as a form of self-making in response to historical times and personal circumstances. William Spengemann, *The Forms of Autobiography* (New Haven, Conn.: Yale University Press, 1980), contains an excellent bibliographical essay on this early work, along with a list of references full enough to gladden a doctoral student's heart. It is worth reading.

Even anthropologists were turning to life narratives to understand how one *becomes* a Zuni or a Kwakiutl. The "new" anthropology, particularly American anthropology, and perhaps in protest against Lévi-Strauss's impersonal structuralism, became preoccupied with "culture and personality," a personal rather than an institutional emphasis. And though at first this work bore the heavy stamp of Freudian theory, in time it came to emphasize the more general question of how human beings create meaning within the framework of their culture. Bronislaw Malinowski became a hero. Margaret Mead and Ruth Benedict became best-sellers. Theirs was an anthropology not just about institutions but about people living their lives. Their anthropology was telling stories about the stories that people told them, putting them in comprehensible genres. Anthropology, in Clifford Geertz's term, became interpretive.

Landmark books, like landmark decisions in the world of law, often provide useful dates for reckoning change. The book in the present case was edited by W. J. T. Mitchell, *On Narrative* (Chicago: University of Chicago Press, 1981), a collection of articles by leading historians, psychoanalysts, philosophers, and literary critics, all of them preoccupied with the new turn. The study of narrative had become a field of its own: its nature, its uses, its significance. And it spread far beyond the academy. Narrative has become almost symbolic: the instrument of the oppressed for battling the hegemony of the ruling elite and their experts, the way to tell one's own story as woman, as ethnic, as dispossessed. Such narrative populism surely reflects the new politics of identity, but that is only part of the story.

2. I borrow this lovely term from Arthur Danto, *The Transfiguration of the Commonplace* (Cambridge, Mass.: Harvard University Press, 1989).

3. This is a rephrase of a discussion in Thomas G. Pavel, *Fictional Worlds* (Cambridge, Mass.: Harvard University Press, 1986), chap. 3. Pavel's is an intriguing discussion of the issue of sense

NOTES

and reference in fiction. It was, of course, the famous late-nineteenth-century essay by Gottlob Frege that brought this distinction back into modern philosophy. See "On Sense and Reference," in *Translations from the Philosophical Writings of Gottlob Frege*, ed. Peter Geach and Max Black (Oxford: Basil Blackwell, 1960).

4. See, for example, Adam Kuper, *Culture: The Anthropologist's Account* (Cambridge, Mass.: Harvard University Press, 1999), where this question is addressed with particular care—and bitterness, Kuper being South African by origin. The general issue of how accounts of culture affect the manner in which we in the "advanced" technological world deal with peoples of different belief systems and origins has exploded with the "scandal of the Yanomami" involving the anthropologist Napoleon Chagnon. See Patrick Tierney, "The Fierce Anthropologist," *New Yorker* (9 October 2000): 50–61; and Clifford Geertz, "Life among the Anthros," *New York Review of Books* (8 February 2001): 18–22.

5. See Roy Schafer, "Narration in the Psychoanalytic Dialogue," in *On Narrative*; and Donald Spence, *Narrative Truth and Historical Truth: Meaning and Interpretation in Psychoanalysis* (New York: W. W. Norton, 1982).

6. For a more extended discussion of "subjunctivizing," see my *Actual Minds, Possible Worlds* (Cambridge, Mass.: Harvard University Press, 1986).

7. Some striking examples of this new genre of scholarship are James Boyd White, *Heracles' Bow: Essays on the Rhetoric and Poetics of the Law* (Madison: University of Wisconsin Press, 1985), and particularly his essay "The Life of the Law as a Life of Writing," in *The Edge of Meaning* (Chicago: University of Chicago Press, 2001); Richard Posner, *Law and Literature: A Misunderstood Relation* (Cambridge, Mass.: Harvard University Press, 1988); *Legal Storytelling*, a special issue of the *Michigan Law Review* 87, no. 8 (1989); and Guyora Binder and Robert Weisberg, *Literary Criticisms of Law* (Princeton, N.J.: Princeton University Press, 2000).

8. The expression "subjunctivizing reality" originated in a discussion of the nature of literary fiction in Tzvetan Todorov, *The Po-*

etics of Prose (Ithaca, N.Y.: Cornell University Press, 1977). I elaborated the idea in comparing James Joyce's fiction with anthropological writing about the origins of the Penitente cult in the American Southwest (see my *Actual Minds, Possible Worlds*), the former abounding in subjunctivizing language and the latter shunning it.

9. Robert Cover, "The Supreme Court 1982 Term: Nomos and Narrative," *Harvard Law Review* 97, no. 4 (1983): 68.

10. Anthony G. Amsterdam and Jerome Bruner, *Minding the Law* (Cambridge, Mass.: Harvard University Press, 2000).

11. I borrow the term "self-making" from Paul John Eakin, whose thoughtful book *How Our Lives Become Stories: Making Selves* (Ithaca, N.Y.: Cornell University Press, 1999) will engage us further in Chapter 3.

12. Michael Tomasello, *The Cultural Origins of Human Cognition* (Cambridge, Mass.: Harvard University Press, 1999).

13. Michael Riffaterre, *Fictional Truth* (Baltimore, Md.: Johns Hopkins University Press, 1990), xv. His book is a deep exploration of how the novelist creates illusions of reality.

14. One of the most thoughtful and penetrating analyses of the shaping role of narrative in historical writing predates (and perhaps sparked) contemporary interest in this subject. It is Louis O. Mink, "Narrative Form as a Cognitive Instrument," in *The Writing of History: Literary Form and Historical Understanding*, ed. R. H. Canary and H. Kozicki (Madison: University of Wisconsin Press, 1978). One could argue that it was Leopold von Ranke's injunction that history is an account of how events are experienced rather than how they "are" *eo ipso* that started the "narrative movement" in history. Surely, the French *Annales* school of historians contributed greatly to our current concern with narrative in history or, perhaps more accurately, history as narrative. As I have noted (in note 1, above), it was Mitchell's *On Narrative* that triggered the interest of historians in narrative; in 2001, twenty years on, the annual meeting of the American Historical Association was given over to the topic "Narrative in History."

15. The example cited comes from Helen Epstein, "Life and Death

on the Social Ladder," an article-review of Richard G. Wilkinson, *Unhealthy Societies: The Afflictions of Inequality,* that appeared in *The New York Review of Books* (16 July 1998): 27–29. It is interesting that in discussing the example, she attempts to fill in the gap between poverty and longevity by citing the somatic afflictions produced by living below the poverty line. Even for a critic of her standing, the epidemic-like impact of poverty is unconvincing unless one can point to its effect on nutrition or disease rates. Yet, to give due credit, she also cites the less "germy" views of Robert Karasek and Töres Theorell, *Healthy Work: Stress, Productivity, and the Reconstruction of Working Life* (New York: Basic Books, 1990), on the stress-producing effects of low-level work conditions.

16. The illocutionary force of an utterance is made clear by an example. The locution "Would you be so kind as to open the window" is not intended as a literal request for information about the limits of your compassion. Rather, it is a request for you to open the window. Speech-act theory, in which the notion of illocutionary force has been developed, is well illustrated in John Searle, *Speech Acts* (Cambridge, U.K.: Cambridge University Press, 1969).

17. See particularly Jean-Pierre Vernant, *Myth and Thought among the Greeks* (London: Routledge, 1983). Though a classicist, Vernant had a powerful effect on the *Annales* school of French historians. It is an interesting footnote on conventional historiography that the group who later founded the *Annales* school served together as Maquis in the French Resistance. Vernant once remarked to me that living in hiding opened the mind to the fragility of all accounts of what was happening, even to the extent of altering one's sense of who and what you were.

18. On this critical point, see Susan Engel, *Context Is Everything* (New York: Freeman, 1999); and Eakin, *How Our Lives Become Stories.*

19. I have spent many hours and much ink on this vexing question, but I remain uneasy with the answers I've come up with, even with how I've gone about the task—as in comparing the narrative mode of thought with the logical-paradigmatic (for

example, in chapter 10 of my *Actual Minds, Possible Worlds*). The approach I shall take here leaves that old comparative method behind, for better or worse!

20. George A. Miller, Karl H. Pribram, and Eugene Galanter, *Plans and the Structure of Behavior* (New York: Holt, Rinehart, Winston, 1960).
21. See Jerome Bruner and Virginia Sherwood, "Early Rule Structure: The Case of 'Peekaboo,' " in *Life Sentences: Aspects of the Social Role of Language*, ed. Rom Harre (New York and London: Wiley, 1976).
22. Jerome Bruner and Joan Lucariello, "Monologue as Narrative Recreation of the World," in *Narratives from the Crib*, ed. Katherine Nelson (Cambridge, Mass.: Harvard University Press, 1989), 73–97.
23. Sue Savage-Rumbaugh, J. Murphy, R. A. Sevcik, K. E. Brakke, S. L. Williams, and Duane Rumbaugh, "Language Comprehension in Ape and Child," *Monographs of the Society for Research in Child Development*, serial no. 233, vol. 58, nos. 3–4 (1993).
24. Burke, *Grammar of Motives*.

TWO: THE LEGAL AND THE LITERARY

1. Adversary stories before a court of law do not, of course, always involve private clients' cases. One party may be pleading the "community's case"—through a public prosecutor representing a municipality, a state, or a nation, with authority to bring an indictment against and/or bring to trial anybody suspected of violating a statute designed to protect the public interest. Or a private citizen may bring suit against the community for violation of rights or other affronts, as in many civil-rights actions. The range of narrative forms increases strikingly in both instances, for each offers an opportunity to the presumably powerful against the presumably powerless—the oppressive state against the encumbered individual, the self-seeking individual against the protective state, and so on. Under the circumstances, history as well as precedent becomes relevant to the stories offered by opposing attorneys.

2. Legal stories, to use a current catchphrase, "name, blame, and claim"—a useful summary of their narrative nature. See W. L. F. Felstiner, R. L. Abel, and A. Sarat, "The Emergence and Transformation of Disputes: Naming, Blaming, and Claiming," *Law and Society Review* 15 (1980): 631–54. That is to say, adversary attorneys specify what they take to be the canonical expectations in matters relating to the case at issue, specify (or deny) the breach of those expectations by the accused party, and then detail what has to be done to right or remedy the breach or to punish the accused. The evaluation and coda of a legal story outdo Aesop in their simplicity: a charge of guilt or a claim of innocence, plus a reiteration of the remedy by the prosecution. For an interesting, rather controversial overview of legal storytelling, see *Legal Storytelling*, a special issue of the *Michigan Law Review* 87, no. 8 (1989).

3. The Supreme Court case cited is *Michael H. v. Gerald D.* 1095 S.Ct. 2333 (1989). For a fuller account, see Anthony G. Amsterdam and Jerome Bruner, *Minding the Law* (Cambridge, Mass.: Harvard University Press, 2000), chap. 3.

4. *Portuondo v. Agard*, 120 S.Ct. 1119 (2000).

5. Plainly, people do have confidence in the law. For a thoughtful study of the basis for this confidence, see Tom R. Tyler, *Why People Obey the Law* (New Haven, Conn.: Yale University Press, 1990). The brunt of Tyler's findings, based on interviews, is that, in fact, people think the courts are fair and treat people in a dignified manner. The book also suggests, though Tyler does not offer it as one of his conclusions, that people, in the main, know very little about legal procedures or about abuses of the law—such matters as plea bargaining, the poor provision of counsel for those who cannot afford their own lawyers, or the racial bias of American courts in dealing with issues of segregation, poverty, and crime.

6. Lon Fuller, *The Morality of Law* (New Haven, Conn.: Yale University Press, 1976).

7. David I. Kertzer, *Ritual, Politics, and Power* (New Haven, Conn.: Yale University Press, 1988), 9.

8. See Catherine Bell's thoughtful analyses of the defining features

of effective ritual in *Ritual Theory, Ritual Practice* (New York: Oxford University Press, 1992) and *Ritual: Perspectives and Dimensions* (New York: Oxford University Press, 1997). See also Victor Turner, *The Ritual Process* (Chicago: Aldine, 1969). Among her criteria, Bell lists formalism, traditionalism, disciplined invariance, rule-governance, sacral symbolism, and performance by participants.

9. See E. E. Evans-Pritchard, *Witchcraft, Oracles, and Magic among the Azande* (Oxford, U.K.: Clarendon Press, 1937). Geertz's classic study is found in his Yale Storrs Lecture, "Local Knowledge: Fact and Law in Comparative Perspective," in *Local Knowledge: Further Essays in Interpretive Anthropology* (New York: Basic Books, 1983), 167–234. See also Sally Falk Moore, "Selection for Failure in a Small Social Field: Ritual Concord and Fraternal Strife among the Chagga, Kilimanjaro, 1968–1969," in *Symbol and Politics in Communal Ideology*, ed. Sally F. Moore and Barbara Myerhoff (Ithaca, N.Y.: Cornell University Press, 1975). There is rich material in Donald Brenneis, "Dramatic Gestures: The Fiji Indian *Pancayat* as Therapeutic Event," in *Disentangling Conflict Discourse in Pacific Societies*, ed. Karen Ann Watson-Gegeo and Geoffrey M. White (Palo Alto, Calif.: Stanford University Press, 1990). Oscar Chase's astute volume, *Culture and Disputing*, is still in preparation. The standard "text" on legal anthropology is Simon Roberts's comprehensive *Order and Dispute: An Introduction to Legal Anthropology* (New York: St. Martin's Press, 1979). Max Gluckman's views can be found in his Yale Storrs Lecture: *The Ideas in Barotse Jurisprudence* (New Haven, Conn.: Yale University Press, 1965).

10. See Robert Cover, "The Supreme Court 1982 Term: Nomos and Narrative," *Harvard Law Review* 97, no. 4 (1983): 4–68. See also his "Violence and the Word," *Yale Law Journal* 95 (1986): 1601–29.

11. Clifford Geertz, *The Interpretation of Cultures* (New York: Basic Books, 1973). Geertz must surely rank as the most cited and most often attacked anthropologist of our era, perhaps by dint of his having recognized so clearly and so early that culture is less an institutional arrangement than a way of interpreting the world in concert with others.

12. See Jack M. Balkin, *What Brown v. Board Should Have Said* (New York: New York University Press, 2001). Among the contributors were Bruce Ackerman, Derrick Bell, Frank Michelman, Catharine MacKinnon, and Cass Sunstein. The review was by Mark Kozlowski in *Legal Times*, 8 October 2001.

13. Anthony FitzHerbert, *New Natura Brevium* (London: Printed for Henry Lintot, Law-Printer to the King's Most Excellent Majesty, 1755).

14. See Amsterdam and Bruner, *Minding the Law*, particularly chaps. 8 and 9.

THREE: THE NARRATIVE CREATION OF SELF

1. See my "The Freudian Conception of Man," *Daedalus* 8, no. 1 (1958): 77–84.

2. See, for example, Donald Spence, *Narrative Truth and Historical Truth: Meaning and Interpretation in Psychoanalysis* (New York: W. W. Norton, 1982); and his development of this theme in *The Freudian Metaphor: Toward Paradigm Change in Psychoanalysis* (New York: W. W. Norton, 1987).

3. Plainly, certain features of selfhood are innate: for example, we locate ourselves posturally at the "zero point" of personal space and time, an ability we share with most mammals. But we rise above that primitive identity almost from the start. Even as young children, we master peekaboo and then go on, once language begins, to the mastery of such daunting tasks as deictic reference: when I say "here" it means something near me; when you say it, it means something near you. My "here" is your "there," a self-switcher found nowhere else in the animal kingdom. How the primitive, postural, and pre-conceptual self is transformed into a conceptual self is interestingly discussed by Ulric Neisser, "Five Kinds of Self-Knowledge," *Philosophical Psychology* 1 (1988): 35–59.

4. See, for example, James Clifford, *The Predicament of Culture* (Cambridge, Mass.: Harvard University Press, 1988); and Adam Kuper, *Culture: The Anthropologist's Account* (Cambridge, Mass.: Harvard University Press, 1999).

5. Philippe Lejeune, *Le Pacte autobiographique* (Paris: Seuil, 1975). See also his later essays in *On Autobiography* (Minneapolis: University of Minnesota Press, 1989).

6. See, for example, Paul Ricoeur, *Oneself as Another* (Chicago: University of Chicago Press, 1962).

7. Eric Gunderson, *Staging Masculinity: The Rhetoric of Performance in the Roman World* (Ann Arbor: University of Michigan Press, 1999).

8. Geoffrey E. R. Lloyd, *Magic, Reason, and Experience* (Cambridge, U.K.: Cambridge University Press, 1979). See also his *Science, Folklore, and Ideology* (Indianapolis: Hackett, 1999). Lloyd also presented an extensive discussion of the classic Greek-Chinese contrast in lectures delivered at the University of Toronto in 1998.

9. For an alarmed and alarming description of the American pattern, see Noelle Oxenhandler, *The Eros of Parenthood* (New York: St. Martin's Press, 2001). It is worth noting that in the half dozen years I have served as a consultant in Italy to the very highly regarded communal preschools (the *scuole dell'infanzia*) of Reggio Emilia, the issue of "showing affection" to children has never been mentioned, while, according to Oxenhandler's account, it is expressly forbidden in the schools and nursery schools of Sonoma County, California, where she lives and works.

10. For an interesting contemporary view of this ongoing debate, see Alan Ryan, "Schools: The Price of 'Progress,'" review of *Left Back: A Century of Failed School Reforms*, by Diane Ravitch, *New York Review of Books* (22 February 2001): 18ff.

11. See Ulric Neisser and Eugene Winograd, eds., *Remembering Reconsidered* (1988); Ulric Neisser, ed., *The Perceived Self* (1993); Ulric Neisser and Robyn Fivush, eds., *The Remembering Self* (1994); Ulric Neisser and David Jopling, *The Conceptual Self in Context* (1997). All these volumes were published by Cambridge University Press.

12. A typical example of this dialogic orientation in self-making can be found in chapter 3 of my *Acts of Meaning* (Cambridge, Mass.: Harvard University Press, 1991). I present there an account of a family discussing the pasts of its members.

13. The anthropologist Richard Shweder argues (on comparative evidence) that there seem to be three normative or "ethical" criteria by which human beings, whatever their culture, judge themselves and others. He believes they relate to "the ethics of autonomy, the ethics of community, and the ethics of divinity." Each has its particularized expression in different cultures, with each given different weightings. So, for example, more communitarian Asian cultures differ from more autonomy-oriented Western cultures, with even the earliest autobiographical memories of Chinese adults containing more community-related self-judging episodes than do the early memories of Americans, the latter tending to remember more episodes related to autonomy. See Richard Shweder, "The Psychology of Practice and the Practice of the Three Psychologies," *Asian Journal of Social Psychology* 3 (2000): 207–22. The data on early autobiographical memories are in Qi Wang, "Culture Effects on Adults' Earliest Childhood Recollection and Self-Description," *Journal of Personality and Social Psychology* 81, no. 2 (2001).

14. While self-telling usually proceeds in ordinary language, ordinary language itself also sports the genres and fashions of its time. Has the so-called inward turn of the novel pulled self-telling inward? What of the lexical "self-explosion" in seventeenth-century England, replete with new reflexive compounds like "self-conscious," "self-reliant," and "self-possessed"? Did those words appear in response to the turbulent century of Hobbes and Locke, Cromwell's Puritan uprising, the dethroning of two Stuart kings, the Glorious Revolution? That is, did the spate of reflexive compounds appear in response to change in the world, and did it alter the way people looked at and told about themselves?

15. Dan I. Slobin, "Verbalized Events: A Dynamic Approach to Linguistic Relativity and Determinism," *Current Issues in Linguistic Theory* 198 (2000): 107. This paper has also been published in *Evidence for Linguistic Relativity*, ed. Susanne Niemeier and René Dirven (Amsterdam and Philadelphia: John Benjamin, 2000).

16. James Olney, *Memory and Narrative: The Weave of Life-Writing* (Chicago: University of Chicago Press, 1998).

17. This is Paul John Eakin's apt phrase. See his *How Our Lives Become Stories: Making Selves* (Ithaca, N.Y.: Cornell University Press, 1999), 45.

18. Inadvertent trauma often produces disruptive and profound turning points in self-narrative, but they are in sharp contrast to these communally supported orderly changes in the *rites de passage*. Trauma typically alienates and isolates those who have suffered it. Victims of rape, for example, are often so consumed by self-blame and guilt that they can scarcely face their community. They are greatly aided by group therapy with other victims, in the course of which they discover that their fellow victims suffer the same sense of isolation as they do.

19. Sigmund Freud, *Delusion and Dream: An Interpretation in the Light of Psychoanalysis of "Gradiva," a Novel by Wilhelm Jensen*, ed. P. Rieff (Boston: Beacon Press, 1956).

20. Eakin, *How Our Lives Become Stories*, 128.

21. Oliver Sacks, *Awakenings* (London: Duckworth, 1973).

22. Oliver Sacks, *The Man Who Mistook His Wife for a Hat and Other Clinical Tales* (New York: Alfred A. Knopf, 1986), 113.

23. Eakin, *How Our Lives Become Stories*, 124, citing Kay Young and Jeffrey L. Saver, "The Neurology of Narrative," paper presented at a session titled "Autobiography and the Neurosciences," Modern Language Association Convention, New York, 29 December 1995.

FOUR: SO WHY NARRATIVE?

1. Victor Turner, *From Ritual to Theatre: The Human Seriousness of Play* (New York: Performing Arts Journal Publications, 1982).

2. Merlin Donald, *Origins of the Modern Mind: Three Stages in the Evolution of Culture and Cognition* (Cambridge, Mass.: Harvard University Press, 1991). See also his *A Mind So Rare: The Evolution of Human Consciousness* (New York: W. W. Norton, 2001).

3. Michael Tomasello, *The Cultural Origins of Human Cognition* (Cambridge, Mass.: Harvard University Press, 1999).

4. See particularly Albert B. Lord, *The Singer of Tales* (Cambridge, Mass.: Harvard University Press, 1960), but also see Vladimir

Propp, *Morphology of the Folktale* (Austin: University of Texas Press, 1968).

5. Paul Veyne, *Did the Greeks Believe in Their Myths?* (Chicago: University of Chicago Press, 1988); E. R. Dodds, *The Greeks and the Irrational* (Berkeley: University of California Press, 1951).

6. Lev S. Vygotsky, *Thought and Language* (Cambridge, Mass.: MIT Press, 1962); see also his *Mind in Society: The Development of Higher Psychological Processes* (Cambridge, Mass.: Harvard University Press, 1978).

7. The new literature on infancy is very rich. An intelligent overview of it, along with a useful bibliography, is in Philippe Rochat, *The Infant's World* (Cambridge, Mass.: Harvard University Press, 2001).

8. Shirley Brice Heath, *Ways with Words: Language, Life, and Work in Communities and Classrooms* (Cambridge, U.K.: Cambridge University Press, 1983).

9. See Franklin D. Gilliam, Jr., and Susan Nall Bales, "Strategic Frame Analysis: Reframing America's Youth," *Social Policy Report* (of the Society for Research in Child Development), 15, no. 3 (2001): 3–14.

10. See Rita Charon, "The Life-Long Error, or John Marcher the Proleptic," in *Margin of Error: The Ethics of Mistakes in the Practice of Medicine*, ed. Susan B. Rubin and Laurie Zoloth (Hagerstown, Md.: University Publishing Group, 2000). Charon uses the example of John Marcher's unwillingness (inability?) to project the past on the future as a model of the unwillingness of attending physicians to use patients' narrative accounts of their illnesses to see their difficulties in coping with the present and future.

11. See Cheryl Mattingly and Linda C. Garro, eds., *Narrative and the Cultural Construction of Illness and Healing* (Berkeley and Los Angeles: University of California Press, 2000); and Cheryl Mattingly, *Healing Dramas and Clinical Plots: The Narrative Construction of Experience* (Cambridge, U.K.: Cambridge University Press, 1998). Closely related to Mattingly's work is Byron J. Good, *Medicine, Rationality, and Experience: An Anthropological Perspective* (Cambridge, U.K.: Cambridge University Press, 1994).

INDEX

INDEX

Hebrews, ancient, 50
Hegel, Georg Wilhelm
    Friedrich, 69
Hemingway, Ernest, *The Sun
    Also Rises*, 7
history, 28–29, 74; *Annales*
    school of, 111*n1*, 114*n14*,
    115*n17*; of epidemics, 23
Hitler, Adolf, 54
Homer, 98, 100
hominids, 96
Hopwood v. *Texas* (1996), 56, 57
Hughes, Langston, 55

Ibsen, Henrik, *A Doll's House*,
    34, 48
immunity, legal, 45
intent: criminal, 69; narrative,
    24–25

Jaeger, Werner, 25
James, Henry, 106
Joyce, James, 49, 61, 114*n8*;
    Dubliners, 51
Judeo-Christian tradition, 68
Justinian, 49–50, 62, 67

Karasek, Robert, 115*n15*
Kerouac, Jack, *On the Road*, 78
Kertzer, David, 45
Korsakov's syndrome, 86
!Kung Bushmen, 83
Kuper, Adam, 113*n4*

Labov, William, 111*n1*
law, 37–62, 93; action and consciousness in, 26–27; adversarial system of, 42–44; Anglo-Saxon common, 58–60;
appellate, 40, 45; attractive
nuisance in, 9; closing arguments in, 41; *corpus juris*, 25,
44, 49, 53, 55–56, 60–62; doctrine of *stare decisis* in, 43, 44;
equal protection under,
53–55, 57, 94; evidence in, 38,
39, 42, 47; Hebrew, 50; intent
in, 25, 69; interpretations in,
21, 39–40; Jim Crow, 54, 55;
jurisgenesis, 50; literature and,
11–13, 39, 48–49, 53, 55, 57,
60, 61; litigation procedures,
38; precedent in, 11, 13, 38,
39, 43, 49, 54, 57, 62, 90; prohibitive statutes, 67–68; racial
discrimination and, 6, 53–58,
93–94; redefinition of past in,
94; revenge and, 37, 46–47;
rituals in, 44–46; self-narrative and, 80–82, 84; standing
in, 41, 43; tort, 9; verdicts in,
37–38; witness testimony in,
41–43; writs in, 58–60, 91
Lee, Harper, *To Kill a Mockingbird*, 34
Lejeune, Philippe, 111*n1*
Lévi-Strauss, Claude, 92, 100,
    110*n1*
life stages, 83, 84
linguistics, 73, 96–97
literature, 6–11, 51–53; action
and consciousness in, 26–27;
art of possible in, 94; autobiographical, 74–78; intent of,
25; law and, 11–13, 39,
48–49, 53, 55, 57, 60, 61;